Best Recipes of Minnesota Inns and Restaurants

Compiled and edited by:
Margaret E. Guthrie

Editorial assistance:
Annie L.J. Saart

II

For additional copies of this book, contact:

Amherst Press
A division of Palmer Publications, Inc.
P.O. Box 296
Amherst, Wisconsin 54406

Table of Contents

Preface...IV

Introduction V

Brunch & Luncheon.. 1

Bread, Rolls, Muffins 15

Appetizers 27

Soups 37

Meat & Poultry 51

Fish & Seafood 73

Vegetables 85

Salads & Salad Dressings.. 95

Desserts... 105

Inns & Restaurants 127

Index 130

Preface

Obviously a book like this one is not the work of one person, even though only one name appears on the cover. There are many people without whom I would not have been able to put this book together.

My acknowledgment of the contribution of others starts with my publisher Chuck Spanbauer, who has been very supportive right from the beginning. I also need to thank my attorney, Michael R. Davis, who ensures that everything always goes smoothly.

For the Minnesota book specifically, thanks go first to Fran and Hammy Hamerstrom for sharing their friends and colleagues with me. Robert Rumpza, my first Minnesota friend, and Marcia Appel, the editor of Twin Cities magazine, who shared restaurant reviews with me, are two others who made life much easier. Donna and Earl Gustafson, hosts extraordinaire, who made my stay in St. Paul so comfortable and easy. Thanks go, too, to area "spies" Dr. Al Grewe of St. Cloud, Dr. P. Hofslund of Duluth and Marjorie Larson of Hopkins.

Most importantly, are all the restaurateurs, innkeepers, and chefs whose recipes were generously shared so that we could all enjoy the wonderful food Minnesota has to offer.

Last, but certainly not least, are my three children who see to it that whatever happens, I keep my sense of humor. I would also like to thank my parents for being tall and thin. It helps.

Thank you all.

Introduction

The public's reception of "The Best Recipes of Wisconsin Inns and Restaurants" was so overwhelming that a series covering the surrounding states immediately became a certainty.

Research for these books confirms that there is a restaurant explosion in this country. And the growth is not all at the fast food end of the restaurant spectrum. The number of cooking and restaurant management schools reflects this, as well as the sheer number of restaurants opening up, the wonderful and eclectic cuisines now available in remote places.

People are more interested in what they eat, more concerned about their health and generally more conscious about food. Women are working outside the home in record numbers. More people have more disposable income. Travel is easier and cheaper than it has ever been. The United States has enjoyed an influx of Southeast Asian peoples who have brought their unique cuisines with them, as have so many other immigrants before them. And with all of this has come a re-discovery of "American" cooking, which truly is a melting pot of other cultures and countries.

Many farmers are turning back to a varied agriculture and offering us wonderful fresh produce and specialty crops that were formerly very difficult to obtain. Local wild produce is also being used by imaginative chefs. One chef, who is from Norway, told me he loved America because he had never seen such a variety of food in his life.

All of this results in the most wonderful Lucullan feast for all us consumers. Even if you are not a person who enjoys going out to eat, you can, through cookbooks like this one, "eat out".

This book reflects the use by imaginative chefs of the local produce. They offer us such delicacies as Wild Rice Soup, Pheasant Pate en Croute, and Lamb Loin in Puff Pastry to name just three.

The work of compiling these cookbooks is made more interesting, if that's possible, by noting the similarities and differences in each state. Most of the similarities are cited above, but there is also an influx of young people into the restaurant business. Young people who have a consuming interest, an abiding passion for good food, well cooked and presented in an attractive and appetizing way.

What varies from state to state are the local ingredients, both wild and domestic. Wisconsin, for instance, vies with Massachusetts in cranberry production and with New York and Vermont in the production of maple syrup. Everyone knows that the best wild rice comes from Minnesota. There's a farmer in Iowa who gave up on corn and soybeans and is raising venison for the restaurant markets. Two farmers in Wisconsin decided they liked goats better than cows and are now producing award winning chevre frais. Michigan produces peaches! And has a flourishing wine industry. All of these discoveries come as a result of working on these books.

It's very exciting to be a participant in this renaissance of cooking and good food here. It's rewarding to set down the work of truly imaginative chefs. This is the only way, other than hearsay, that a chef's work lives on for the enjoyment of others. After all, if a chef is really good, there's nothing left but an empty plate.

Finally, I would just pass along what several of the chefs have said to me. If you want to achieve the results you tasted in the restaurant, or you just want the recipe to succeed, follow the instructions carefully and do *not* substitute ingredients. If the recipe calls for Dijon mustard, do not use American yellow. If a specific ingredient is called for, there's good reason for it. Taste, texture, cooking time, appearance, all of these are involved. So, if a recipe specifies a certain ingredient, use it, don't substitute. After all, these women and men are professionals.

The only advice I would add to that is to sit down and read the recipe all the way through before you begin. Be sure you have all the necessary ingredients, be sure you understand the steps and the order in which you're to do things.

Bon Appetit.

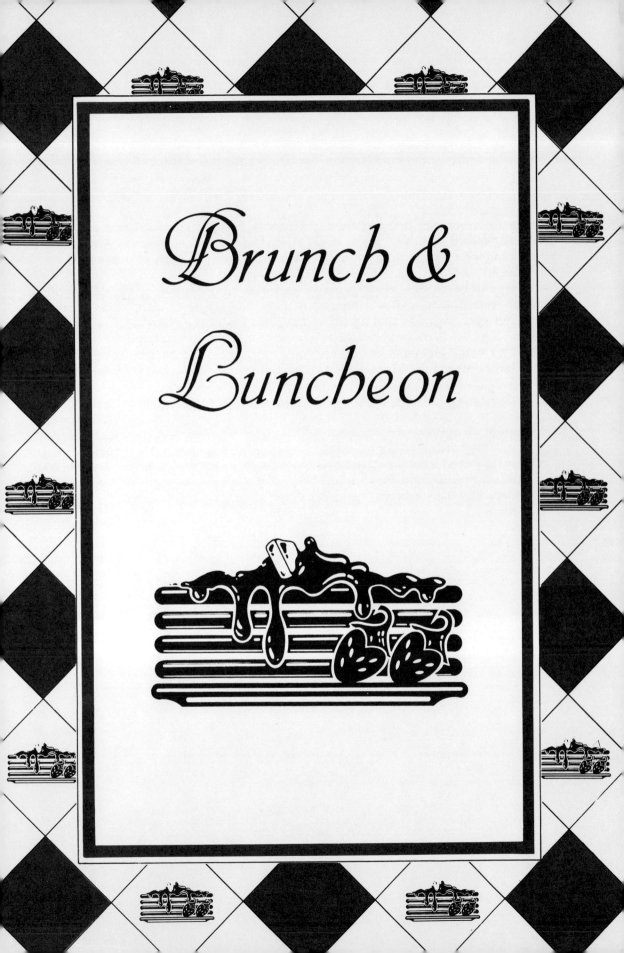

Brunch & Luncheon

Brunch & Luncheon

Brunch has become an increasingly popular meal on the weekends, due in large part to the very busy, active lives we all lead. Brunch affords a chance to get together over a leisurely meal that is not going to break the bank or the waistline.

Combining the best elements of breakfast and lunch, you can eat just about anything that appeals to you. Restaurants that "do" brunch cater to this taste and usually offer a wide selection ranging from pancakes and omelets to fish, seafood and meats.

Due to the interest in northern Italian cooking you will find several pasta dishes in this chapter. The Italians serve pasta at lunch, but also as a separate course between antipasto and entree, which they call I Secondi. The pasta course is called I Primi. According to one authority on Italian cooking, most of the genius of Italian chefs goes into I Primi.

Brunch is as good a way to entertain as it is a way to dine out. Besides giving you a free range to express your culinary talents, you don't have to worry about the guest who ends up staying too late. Since brunch is late morning, early afternoon, everyone should have gone home in time for you to watch the evening news on television.

Brunch is also a good way to entertain around something—like cross-country skiing, the Super Bowl, whatever an abiding interest is that you share with friends.

Minnesota's chefs herewith offer you everything from Kamikaze Pancakes to Linguini con Vongole. Salut.

Five Star Brunch

12 slices good, homestyle bread,
  crusts removed
3 Tbsps. butter
½ cup butter
½ lb. fresh mushrooms
2 cups yellow onions,
  thinly sliced
salt & pepper to taste
1½ lbs. mild Italian bulk sausage
¾ lb. Cheddar cheese, grated
5 eggs
2½ cups milk
2 Tbsps. Dijon mustard
2 Tbsps. chopped parsley

Spread bread with 3 tablespoons butter and set aside. Melt ½ cup butter in a large, heavy skillet and brown mushrooms and onions over medium heat until tender. Season to taste with salt and pepper and set aside. Cook sausage, breaking up with a fork in small pieces.

In a buttered, shallow 11″ x 17″ pan, layer half the bread, mushroom mixture, sausage and cheese. Repeat the layers. In medium size mixing bowl, beat together the eggs, milk, mustard, salt and pepper to taste. Pour over baking dish and refrigerate overnight. When ready to bake, sprinkle parsley over top, if desired, and bake uncovered for one hour in a preheated 350-degree oven. Yield: 8 servings.

From: **The Anderson House**
          333 West Main Street
          Wabasha, Minnesota

Goatmilk Yogurt Pancakes

These pancakes are tender, light and tasty!

2 eggs, beaten
2½ cups yogurt*
2½ cups flour,
  or other grains to your taste
4 Tbsps. oil
2 tsps. sugar
2 tsps. baking powder

Beat eggs well, then add other ingredients until well mixed. Cook on griddle.

*To make the yogurt, take 1 quart goat milk warmed to 100 degrees and add ½ cup plain yogurt. Mix together, set in lightly covered glass dish in oven with pilot light overnight. If you have an electric stove, turn

1 tsp. baking soda
1 tsp. salt

oven to 200 degrees. When oven reaches that temperature, turn off and put yogurt in oven. Or use an electric yogurt maker. If you don't want to bother with all this, just use plain yogurt. The flavor and light tenderness is reduced, however. Buttermilk will work, too. Serve with berries, fried apples or nuts.

From: **Mrs. B's Historic Lanesboro Inn**
101 Parkway
Lanesboro, Minnesota

Kamikaze Pancakes

Kamikaze pancakes have gone over *big* with our customers. They are very simple to make.

blueberries
pecans
bananas

Mix together. The amount depends on the number you have to serve.

Using your favorite pancake recipe—we use whole-wheat, buttermilk, or sourdough pancakes—pour batter on the griddle. Add Kamikaze mixture. When done on one side, flip over. When done, serve with Kamikaze topping.

Kamikaze Topping

1 cup plain yoghurt
bananas
blueberries
pecans

Mix together and top Kamikaze pancakes. Serve.

From: **The Egg and I**
2704 Lyndale Avenue S.
Minneapolis, Minnesota

Broccoli Quiche

1 9" pie crust
½ lb. broccoli, diced
½ cup onion, diced
6 oz. Swiss cheese, shredded
4 eggs, beaten
1 pt. heavy cream

Saute broccoli and onion in 2-3 tablespoons butter. Using slotted spoon put in pie crust. Top with shredded cheese.

Beat eggs with cream and pour over cheese vegetable mixture. Bake in a preheated 350-degree oven for approximately 30 minutes or until firm. Allow 5-8 minutes to set up before cutting. Yield: serves 6-8.

From: **The Pirate's Cove**
7215 N.E. River Road
Sauk Rapids, Minnesota

Capellini con Gamberetti

24 oz. fresh, or 1 lb. dry capellini
  (angel hair pasta)
6 oz. olive oil
15 oz. salad shrimp, thawed
2 tomatoes, chopped
6 Tbsps. fresh basil, chopped
2 Tbsps. garlic, chopped
salt to taste
white pepper to taste
1 tsp. lemon juice
lemon wedges

Cook pasta until al dente (just done and still firm) in boiling water. Immediately drain (reserve water and hold hot) pasta and run under cold water until cold. Toss cold pasta in 2 oz. of olive oil. Drain off excess oil.

Heat 4 oz. olive oil in a saute pan. When oil is hot add shrimp, tomato, basil, garlic, salt and white pepper. Cook until all ingredients are hot, reduce heat and add lemon juice.

Reheat pasta in hot water for about 20 seconds, drain thoroughly. Add pasta to saute pan and toss quickly with sauteed

shrimp, etc. Serve on warm plates. Garnish
with lemon wedge.

From: **Figlio's**
          3001 Hennepin Avenue
          Minneapolis, Minnesota

Chicken Breast in a Package

For each serving:

1 boned chicken breast,
   pressed flat
2 Tbsps. melted butter
1 oz. Boursin cheese*
3 sheets of phyllo dough**

Flatten chicken breast between 2 sheets of
waxed paper. Cut phyllo sheets in half and
spread each with melted butter while stack-
ing them. Don't stack squarely, but rotate
them so you have many points.

Place chicken breast on top and put Boursin cheese on chicken. Gather phyllo around
the chicken breast, making a package with a
frilly top. Bake in preheated 375-degree oven
for 40-45 minutes. Yield: 1 serving.

*Boursin is a soft cheese most often found in gourmet food shops. Rondele is an
acceptable substitute, usually found in the dairy case of good supermarkets.

**Phyllo dough can be purchased frozen and you can usually purchase it in
good supermarkets.

From: **Treats, Ltd.**
            The Archer House
            212 Division Street
            Northfield, Minnesota

Chili with Beef, Pork & Chicken

¼ cup olive oil
1 lb. trimmed, cubed sirloin
1 lb. trimmed, cubed
    pork shoulder
1 lb. trimmed, cubed
    dark meat chicken
1 large onion, coarsely chopped
3 cups tomatoes,
    peeled & chopped
1 bottle dark beer
2 Tbsps. Hungarian paprika
1 Tbsp. salt
1 Tbsp. ground cumin
1½ tsps. leaf oregano
1 ½ tsps. ground coriander
2 jalapeno peppers,
    seeded & minced
1 green pepper, chopped
1 red pepper, chopped
1 yellow pepper, chopped

Put olive oil in a large pan, saute the sirloin, pork and chicken till browned. Add the onion and cook until soft. Add tomatoes, beer, all the dry spices and the jalapeno peppers. Simmer over a low heat for about an hour. Add the bell peppers and simmer another 20 minutes. Serve with a crusty French bread or corn bread.

From: **W.A. Frost & Co.**
374 Selby Avenue
St. Paul, Minnesota

Clam Linguini

2 cups heavy cream
2 cups half & half
2 cups white wine
½ cup sherry
½ cup water
½ cup chopped fresh parsley
2 cups chopped clams,
    frozen or canned, use juice
1½ Tbsps. thyme leaves
4 ozs. clam base
2 tsps. crushed garlic

Put the creams, wines, water, garlic, thyme, parsley, clams and juice, and base into a large, heavy saucepan and simmer for 15 minutes.

While this is cooking, melt the butter for roux and add flour. Stir, cooking for several minutes, then add to the sauce mixture.

Cook 2 pounds linguini according to package directions until al dente which means to spring back when pulled. If in doubt, throw a piece against the wall—if it sticks, it's ready. Add the linguini to the sauce and serve.

Roux:
⅓ lb. butter
⅓ lb. flour
(1 cup plus ½ tsp.)

Yield: 6-8 servings. Sauce may be made 3 or 4 days in advance and refrigerated.

From: **Muffuleta in the Park**
2260 Como Avenue
St. Paul, Minnesota

Linguini con Vongole

3 lbs. Littleneck or
Cherrystone clams
1 cup white wine
1 medium onion, finely diced
4 cloves garlic, minced
¼ cup parsley, minced
¼ cup fresh thyme, minced
2 lemons, juiced
2 oz. clarified butter
1 qt. heavy cream
salt to taste
white pepper to taste
1 lb. dry linguini

Steam clams in white wine. Reserve juice. Remove clams from shells, leaving 6-8 clams for garnish. Chop clams into small pieces and set aside.

Saute onion and garlic in butter until onion is transparent. Add clam juice, lemon juice and reduce by half. Add thyme and cream and reduce by half. Add clams, parsley, and seasoning.

Cook linguini in boiling, salted water until al dente. To test for doneness, a piece of linguini may be thrown against cupboard door. If it sticks, it's ready. Toss cooked pasta with clam sauce and garnish with steamed clams left in shell. Yield: 6-8 portions.

From: **Alfredo's**
Park Square Court
400 Sibley Street
St. Paul, Minnesota

Ragout of Lobster
and Seasonal Vegetables

6 oz. lobster meat
8 asparagus tips, 1½"
6 trimmed zucchini
4 mini carrots
3 oz. haricots verts*
6 snow pea pods
1/2 oz. clarified butter
5 oz. lobster stock
2 Tbsps. butter
salt & white pepper to taste

Cut the lobster into bite size pieces no larger than 1". Trim the zucchini into oval shapes, keeping them the size of the carrots. Trim the ends of the beans and peas. Cut the asparagus tips, reserving the mid-sections for other uses. Wash all the vegetables.

Bring salted water to a boil (½ tsp. salt to 1 qt. water) and in it blanch zucchini, carrots, beans and asparagus tips for 3 minutes and immediately quench them in ice cold water for 5 minutes. Drain and add them together with the snow peas.

Heat the clarified butter in a saute pan over very high heat. When the butter is extremely hot, add the lobster and toss for 5 seconds and add the vegetables and toss for 15-30 seconds before adding the stock.

After adding the stock, allow the stock to boil for 3-5 minutes. Once the stock has reduced by one fourth or so, turn the heat to low and fold the cold butter in. Salt and pepper to taste. Yield: 1 serving.

*Note—haricots vert are French green beans, longer and thinner than their American counterparts. The best place to look for them is at farmer's markets. If you can't find them substitute fresh American green beans.

From: **Primavera**
The Atrium
International Market Square
275 Market Street
Minneapolis, Minnesota

Lobster Stock

10 lobster shells
8 oz. clarified butter
1 onion, chopped
1 carrot, chopped
1 leek, chopped
2 tomatoes, chopped
2 Tbsps. tomato paste
4 oz. Congnac or brandy
3 cups white wine
2 qts. chicken stock
1 Tbsp. fresh tarragon
1 cup heavy cream

In a 10-quart stock pot, heat the butter until very hot, add lobster shells. Stir, cooking for 5-8 minutes until shells become very red in color. Add vegetables, including the tomato paste and toss until coated with butter. Then add the Cognac and let the alcohol fumes evaporate.

Add the remaining ingredients and simmer for 2-3 hours.

Strain the mixture, pushing down on the lobster shells to extract all of the stock. Reduce the stock to 1 quart to intensify the flavor. Store in a covered container.

From: **Primavera**
The Atrium
International Market Square
275 Market Street
Minneapolis, Minnesota

Poppy Seed Spatzle

3 cups flour
3 eggs
¾ tsp. salt
¼ tsp. pepper
½ tsp. nutmeg
½ cup poppy seeds
1 cup milk

Make a well in the center of the flour and drop in the eggs, spices and poppy seeds. Add milk and knead. Batter should go through holes in your colander.

Press the batter through the holes in the colander with the back of a wooden spoon, while nesting the colander over a kettle of boiling salted water. The spatzle will rise to the top when done and can be skimmed off, buttered well and kept hot in a heavy bowl in the oven while other dishes are finished.

From: **Mrs. B's Historic
Lanesboro Inn**
101 Parkway
Lanesboro, Minnesota

Ravioli con Zucca

*Rectangular pasta sheets**

2 whole acorn squash
cinnamon to taste
nutmeg to taste
1 pt. heavy cream
4 oz. freshly grated
  Parmesan cheese
2 oz. butter
2 oz. hazelnuts

*The best recipe and directions for pasta are contained in "The Joy of Cooking."

Cut squash in half and remove seeds. Place cut side down in baking dish with a little water to prevent sticking. Bake squash in 350-degree oven until done. Scoop out flesh and puree as for mashed potatoes. Add cinnamon and nutmeg to flavor. Refrigerate.

Roll out one pasta sheet for ravioli. Partly score the sheet in 2" or 3" squares. Put 2 or 3 teaspoons of squash filling in each square. Place second sheet over first, pressing down on all four sides around each lump of filling. Using a pie crust or pizza wheel, cut along the lengthwise edges to help seal the dough. Then cut across, separating each ravioli. Place on rack and allow ravioli to dry.

Have a pot of boiling, salted water ready. Drop the ravioli, a few at a time, into the water, careful not to disturb the boiling. Ravioli will float to the top when done.

Heat the cream with the butter and stir in the Parmesan cheese. Add salt and pepper to taste. Toss the drained, cooked raviolis in the sauce, garnish with chopped hazelnuts and serve.

From: **Pronto Ristorante**
Hyatt Regency Hotel
Minneapolis, Minnesota

Vegetarian Stuffed Peppers

Served with tomato sauce and poached or fried eggs for brunch, luncheon or supper

6 large bell peppers, green,
  yellow or red, or a combination
3 cups cooked brown rice
3 Tbsps. chopped onion
2 tsps. chopped garlic
¼ cup olive oil
½ cup very hearty whole wheat
  bread crumbs
1 tsp. capers, rinsed & drained
2 Tbsps. raisins,
  plumped in hot water, drained
8 imported black olives,
  seeded, rinsed & chopped*
½ cup chopped walnuts
2 Tbsps. chopped fresh
  sweet basil (or 2 tsps. dry)
¼ cup fresh parsley, chopped,
  do not use dried
1 tsp. orange zest
½ cup orange juice
1 egg

*Note: Do not use California olives in this recipe.

Blanch peppers in boiling water or microwave them to tenderize. Cut peppers in half lengthwise, leaving stem intact. Remove seeds and membrane. Peppers should be somewhat firm. Set aside.

Saute onions and garlic in olive oil until translucent. Combine onion/garlic mixture, rice, crumbs, capers, raisins, walnuts, sweet basil, parsley and finely chopped zest. Mix egg with orange juice and toss with filling. Taste for salt—olives and capers are both salty and depending on you palate, additional salt may not be necessary.

Mound filling in pepper halves and place halves filling side up in a baking dish. Put ½ cup water in dish and cover with lid or foil. Bake for 45 minutes in a preheated 350-degree oven. Yield: 6 servings.

From: **Pam Sherman's
Bakery and Cafe**
2914 Hennepin Avenue
Minneapolis, Minnesota

Tomato Sauce

1 lb. fresh tomatoes,
peeled & seeded or
1 cup canned tomatoes & juice
⅓ cup chopped carrot
⅓ cup chopped celery
⅓ cup chopped onion
¼ tsp. sugar
⅓ cup olive oil

Seed tomatoes and reserve all juices. If using fresh tomatoes, cook in a covered sauce pan for 10 minutes over medium heat. If using canned tomatoes, eliminate the 10 minute pre-cooking time. Add all other ingredients and cook at a steady simmer for 30 minutes, uncovered. Coarsely puree through a food mill or in a blender. Do not make mixture homogenous—you should be able to detect bits of the various vegetables. Return to heat for another 15 minutes. Taste for salt.

From: **Pam Sherman's Bakery & Cafe**
2914 Hennepin Avenue
Minneapolis, Minnesota

Bread, Rolls, Muffins

Bread, Rolls, Muffins

There's a hoary old saying that bread is the staff of life. While that may or not be true any longer, I know of no one who does not like bread in some form. Most of us like it in a variety of forms.

The revival of interest in food and how it's cooked, the importation of different cuisines to this country, and the sheer bounty this country offers, have all led to a bread renaissance and led away from the dull, flabby, plain white bread, we remember as children. So here's to bread, rolls, muffins, and scones in all their tastes and textures.

Plum Biscuits

2 cups flour
4 Tbsps. baking powder
4 Tbsps. sugar
pinch of salt
grated rind of 1 lemon
1 egg yolk, beaten
½ cup cream
3 Tbsps. butter, heaping

Red or blue plums
   halved and pitted

Sift together dry ingredients. Add butter, cut into little bits and cut into dry ingredients with pastry blender or two knives. When consistency of cornmeal, add egg yolk which has been beaten in the cream.

Roll dough out about 1″ thick. If dough is inclined to be a little soft, additional flour may be sprinkled on and worked in to give the necessary firmness.

Cut with large size biscuit cutter (3″). Make a depression in the center of each biscuit and place a half of a plum, inside up, in the depression. Sprinkle top of biscuit with sugar and fill the inside of each half plum with about 1 teaspoon of sugar. If plums are very ripe, sugar may be reduced. Sprinkle with a very little lemon juice to bring out the flavor of the plums. Dot with butter and bake in a moderate over (350 degrees) for 30-45 minutes, or until plums are done.

From: **The Anderson House**
333 West Main Street
Wabasha, Minnesota

Lemon Cream Nut Bread

The bread tray at the Anderson House has many kinds of breads and rolls on it. Among the favorites are the lemon breads.

2½ cups flour
1 Tbsp. baking powder
1 tsp. salt
1⅓ cups sugar
½ cup butter
2 eggs
8 oz. cream cheese, cut up
   in ¼" pieces
1 cup milk
½ cup chopped pecans
2 Tbsps. grated lemon peel

Glaze:
⅓ cup sugar
¼ cup lemon juice

Sift flour with baking powder and salt. Add sugar to butter and cream with mixer at high speed. Blend in the eggs and add dry ingredients. Fold in the cream cheese cubes, milk, nuts and lemon peel.

Pour batter into well greased loaf pan and bake at 375 degrees for about 50 minutes. Remove from oven to metal rack. Pour glaze over the top while still hot. Brush evenly with pastry brush. Cool 30 minutes before removing from pan and slicing. Yield: 1 loaf.

From: **The Anderson House**
333 West Main Sreet
Wabasha, Minnesota

Swiss Pear Bread

1 lb. dried prunes
1 lb. dried apricots
1 lb. dried pears

½ lb. raisins
½ lb. currants
½ lb. citron
½ lb. orange peel
½ lb. lemon peel
1 Tbsp. cinnamon
½ tsp. ground cloves
½ oz. anise

Sponge:
6-8 cups flour
1½ cups sugar
1 Tbsp. salt
4 cups fruit juice
½ lb. yeast
2 Tbsps. butter, melted
1 wine glass brandy

Cook the dried prunes, pears and apricots separately, according to package directions. Reserve the juice for the sponge and put fruit through a meat grinder.

Mix together the raisins, currants, citron, peels and spices. Add to the ground fruit.

Sift flour, sugar and salt together. Gradually add fruit juice, yeast mixture, melted butter and brandy. When thoroughly blended, add fruit mixture. Knead dough until it is stiff, adding flour if necessary. Dough should be shiny and not stick to board.

Place in a greased bowl, cover with a clean cloth and leave in a draft free place overnight. Shape into loaves and let rise about two hours. Bake 15 minutes in a preheated 450-degree oven until brown. Turn oven to 350 degrees and bake another hour. Yield: 6-8 loaves.

From: **The Lowell Inn**
102 North Second Street
Stillwater, Minnesota

Italian Pepper and Crackling Bread

¾ lb. salt pork
6 cups all purpose flour,
    divided
2 Tbsps. dry yeast
¼ cup sugar
4 tsps. basil leaves, crumbled
1½ tsps. black pepper
    freshly ground
1½ cups warm water

Cut skin pieces from pork; dice into ⅛" pieces. Place pork in medium skillet; cook over moderate heat until browned and crisp. Remove cracklings (pork bits) from fat; set aside. Reserve 3 tablespoons of fat for later use. In large bowl of an electric mixer, combine 3 cups of flour, yeast, sugar, basil and black pepper. Add water and reserved 2 tablespoons of fat. Mix at low speed until blended. Mix at high speed for 3 minutes. With a wooden spoon, stir in pork bits and enough remaining flour to make a smooth dough, about 2 cups.

Turn dough onto lightly floured board; knead in enough remaining flour to make a stiff dough (about 1 cup). Place in a greased bowl; turn so greased side is up. Cover and let rise in a warm, draft free place until doubled in bulk, about 45 minutes. Punch dough down. Cut into 3 equal parts. On a lightly floured board, roll each part into a 10" x 12" rectangle. Roll up jelly roll fashion. Shape into a circle; overlap ends to fasten. Place on greased cookie sheets. Brush lightly with remaining 1 tablespoon reserved fat. Cover and let rise in a warm place until double in bulk, about 30 minutes. Bake in a preheated, moderate oven at 375 degrees until bread sounds hollow when rapped with a knuckle, about 30 minutes. Cool on wire racks. Makes 3 loaves.

From: **The Anderson House**
333 West Main Street
Wabasha, Minnesota

Limpa Bread

2 Tbsps. dry yeast
3 ½ cups warm water
¼ cup granulated sugar
½ cup brown sugar
1 Tbsp. salt
¼ lb. lard, melted
½ cup molasses
2 ½ lbs. white bread flour
10 oz. rye flour
2 oz. whole caraway seed
2 ¼ cups minced fresh orange

Dissolve yeast in a bowl in the warm water. Add sugars, salt, melted lard and molasses; mix well. Add flours, caraway seed and orange.

Knead until smooth, adding more white flour if necessary to obtain a stiff dough. After mixing, let rest in a warm place until dough doubles in size, about 1½ hours. Form into 6 (1 pound) round loaves. Let rise again until doubled in size.

Cut slits across the top, brush with an egg wash made with 1 egg beaten with 1 tablespoon of water. Bake in a preheated 390 degree oven for 30 minutes or until loaves sound hollow when rapped with a knuckle. Yield: 6 loaves.

From: **The Grant House**
Fourth and Bremer
Box 87
Rush City, Minnesota

Swedish Rye Raisin Bread

2 Tbsps. dry yeast
½ cup warm water
¾ cup dark molasses
1 cup raisins
2 Tbsps. salt
⅓ cup brown sugar
6 cups warm water
10+ cups white bread flour
⅓ cup melted lard
3 cups rye flour

Put yeast in small bowl with warm water. Put molasses, raisins, salt, brown sugar and 6 cups of warm water in the large bowl of an electric mixer. When the yeast begins working, add it to the molasses mixture. Add most of the white flour and stir until mixture thickens. Add the melted shortening, which has been allowed to cool. Add rye flour. Stir and add remaining white flour until dough no longer sticks to hands and forms around the beater in the bowl.

Place in a bowl that has been greased, turning to let greased side up. Cover with a cloth and put in a warm place. When dough has doubled in bulk, punch down, remove from bowl and form into loaves. Let rise again. Bake in a preheated, moderate 375-degree oven for 20 minutes, then turn oven down to 350 degrees for last 20 minutes.

Yield: 6 loaves.

From: **East Bay Hotel**
Grand Marais, Minnesota

Crescent Rolls

2 Tbsps. dry yeast
1 cup warm water
¼ cup sugar
1 Tbsp. salt
1 cup warm milk
7-8 cups flour
3 eggs
¼ cup melted butter

Put yeast in small bowl with warm water. Sprinkle with a little sugar. Dissolve the ¼ cup sugar and salt in warm milk, add 2-3 cups flour. Mix in eggs, then yeast mixture, then melted butter. Add remaining flour, mixing until stiff but soft.

Turn into greased bowl, turning dough so greased side is up. Cover with cloth and let rise until double in bulk. Punch down and let rise again, turn out on floured board and let rest 10 minutes. Roll and shape into crescents, place on greased cookie sheets.

Bake in preheated oven at 400 degrees for 10-15 minutes, until golden brown. Yield: 50 rolls.

From: **The Lowell Inn**
102 North Second Street
Stillwater, Minnesota

Currant Scones

¼ cup butter
2 cups + 2 Tbsps. flour
1½ Tbsps. baking powder
pinch salt
¾ cup buttermilk
2 Tbsps. sugar
½-¾ cup currants

Mix together, using fingertips, the butter, flour, baking powder and salt. Mixture should resemble cornmeal.

Make a well in center and dump in the buttermilk and sugar. Dough should be soft. Add currants. Do not soak in water before adding to dough. Knead dough and divide into 2 balls. Roll out into circles about ¾-1" thick.

Place the rolled circles on large baking sheets. Wash surfaces of dough with egg white/water wash and sprinkle with sugar. Score or partially cut into pie shaped wedges about 1½" wide at perimeter of circles. Let rest for 15 minutes at room temperature. Preheat oven to 425 degrees, then place pans on other pans in oven to prevent excessive bottom browning. Bake only until lightly browned on top, 10-15 minutes. Break apart or cut at wedge lines and serve hot. Serve with sweetened butter.

From: **Mrs. B's Historic Lanesboro Inn**
101 Parkway
Lanesboro, Minnesota

Sweetened Butter

½ cup butter, softened
3 oz. cream cheese, softened
½ cup powdered sugar
1 Tbsp. fresh orange zest,
  lemon zest or ground nuts

Blend and chill to keep. Serve at room temperature.

From: **Mrs. B's Historic Lanesboro Inn**
101 Parkway
Lanesboro, Minnesota

Cinnamon Honey Butter

1 lb. butter
½ cup honey
1 Tbsp. cinnamon

The butter must be at room temperature. Do not attempt to use a butter substitute or margarine as it will not work.

Using a mixer, whip the butter until it is light and airy. Slowly add the cinnamon and honey, continuing to mix until well blended.

Serve with freshly baked bread, muffins or the pastry of your choice.

From: **Clyde's on the St. Croix**
Bayport, Minnesota

25

Van's Garlic Toast

1 loaf French bread,
cut into slices 1 "thick
½ lb. butter, melted
pinch garlic salt.

Melt butter, add a little garlic salt.

Dip each slice into butter and squeeze out excess. Place on cookie sheet. Sprinkle with more garlic salt. Bake in preheated 450-degree oven until golden brown. Turn, sprinkle garlic salt, and brown other side.

Let air dry, when ready to serve, heat at 190 degrees for about 10 minutes.

From: **Stable's Supper Club**
Richway Drive, West
Albert Lea, Minnesota

Appetizers

Appetizers

Just the word appetizers lets you know you're in for something special. Something to tease the palate and awaken your appetite: now, that's something to look forward to and with good reason as these recipes will show.

Often an appetizer served with a good wine is a meal in and of itself. As a prelude it's all important, since it sets the tone for the meal. These appetizers live up to any expectation, I think you'll agree.

Gravad Lox

This recipe is Swedish in derivation.

5 lbs. salmon filets
(have fish dealer filet the fish)
2 Tbsps. salt
2 Tbsps. crushed black
peppercorns
1 cup sugar
1 cup fresh dill, roughly chopped
½ cup fennel seeds
4 cups salad oil

Place salmon filets in deep dish, just large enough to hold the fish. Sprinkle fish with the salt, pepper, sugar, dill and fennel seed. Pack these ingredients into the flesh of the fish to let the spices seep through. Cover with salad oil and marinate in the refrigerator for three days.

To serve, carefully brush off some of the spices and seasonings. Starting at tail, slice fish crosswise into paper-thin but uniform pieces. Arrange on pumpernickel bread and serve with mustard dill sauce.

Mustard Dill Sauce

1 cup Dijon mustard
½ cup sugar or honey
½ cup white wine vinegar
2 cups salad oil
1 cup fresh chopped dill

Combine mustard with sugar and blend together with the fresh dill. Stir in vinegar and oil and mix thoroughly. Refrigerate.

From: **L'Etoile Restaurant**
The St. Paul Hotel
350 Market Street
St. Paul, Minnesota

Kofta

This recipe is Afghani.

2 lbs. ground lamb
6 whole black peppercorns
6 cloves
6 caraway seeds
½ cup dried yellow peas
1 cup chopped onions
2 eggs

10 hard boiled eggs

Blend all of the ingredients except the eggs and the hard boiled eggs. Cover the mixture with boiling water and cook until peas are tender and the water has boiled away.

Allow the mixture to cool, then work into a fine paste, adding the 2 eggs. Cut the 10 hard boiled eggs in half widthwise, wrap the meat paste around each half egg.

Fry each in oil until brown. Remove from the oil and place the kofta in a gravy made by frying 1 pound (2 cups) of onions chopped fine in oil until brown. Add 1 teaspoon of red pepper, 1 teaspoon of salt and 2 cups water to the onions and bring to a boil.

From: **Caravan Serai**
2046 Pinehurst Avenue
St. Paul, Minnesota

Moules Marniere

4 lbs. mussels
2 cups white wine
1 oz. chopped shallots
1 cup cream
1 oz. butter
salt and pepper to taste

Using a knife, scrape off the barnacles, etc. sticking to the shells, as well as the beards. Swish them around in water energetically to rid them of sand. Then drain. Do not leave them very long in the water, since they might open and lose some of their sea water.

Put the mussels in a heavy saucepan. Add the wine, shallots, parsley, the butter, the cream, salt and pepper. Cook covered for a few minutes until all the shells are open. Serve.

From: **Chez Colette**
L'Hotel Sofitel
5601 West 78th Street
Bloomington, Minnesota

Pheasant Pâté en Croute

1 lb. fresh pork fat back
1 cup cubed boneless pheasant
½ cup cubed lean veal
½ cup cubed lean pork
¾ cup heavy cream
1 Tbsp. salt
1 Tbsp. white pepper
4 oz. cognac or brandy
1 Tbsp. pâté spice
   (finely ground thyme,
   marjoram, allspice, nutmeg)
2 Tbsps. diced truffles,
   roughly chopped

2 lbs. prepared basic
   pâté brise dough*
2 cups prepared liquid gelatin,
   flavored with port wine
1 14" x 2" x 2" pate form
¼ cup beaten egg yolks

*NOTE: Pâté brise dough or short dough is a special pastry devoloped by the French. It's especially good for meat pies or dishes with a high moisture content. An excellent recipe for pâté brise is found in the "Joy of Cooking."

Preheat oven to 375 degrees.

Cut ½ pound pork fat back into cubes. Put fat, one half of the cubed pheasant, all of the veal and pork through food grinder. Puree this mixture in food processor or blender, adding the heavy cream a little at a time until texture is smooth and pasty. Place in mixing bowl and chill for approximately 30 minutes. Then add the salt, pepper, pate spice, truffles, and pistachios, mixing thoroughly and adding cognac a little at a time. Dice remaining pheasant meat, add to pate mixture and refrigerate.

With rolling pin, roll pâté brise dough out on on floured board to a thickness no less than ⅛". Cut dough into proper sizes for lining mold. Press dough all around the walls and bottom of the mold. Dough should overlap the mold's edges by about ½". Overlapping dough will seal the lid later. Slice the remaining pork fat into paper-thin slices and line bottom and sides of mold. Fill mold with refrigerated meat mixture or forcemeat. Press this forcemeat firmly into place so there are no air pockets. Cover this with the sliced pork fat. Cut a remaining piece of dough into the same shape as mold top. Moisten the dough edge with egg yolks and seal top of mold. In the center, make a circular hole called a chimney, to allow steam to escape while baking. A piece of parchment paper rolled into a tube should be inserted into this chimney.

Bake pâté approximately 45 minutes until dough is golden brown and meat well done. Cool one hour before refrigerating. When thoroughly chilled, fill the cavity on top with liquid gelatin. Chill again until set. Carefully remove pate from mold and cut into uniform slices. Serve with Cumberland Sauce. Yield: 12 servings.

Cumberland Sauce

½ cup red currant jelly
2 oz. port wine
¼ cup orange juice
2 Tbsps. orange & lemon peel
(optional) grated
¼ tsp. English mustard
1 pinch ground ginger
1 tsp. finely chopped shallots

Combine currant jelly, port wine, and orange thoroughly. If the consistency is too thin, add more jelly to obtain a thick sauce. Add remaining ingredients, mix well and chill. Serve with Pheasant Pate.

From: **L'Etoile Restaurant**
The St. Paul Hotel
350 Market Street
St. Paul, Minnesota

Cornet of Salmon "Ciboulette"

12 oz. thinly sliced,
  smoked salmon
  (approx. 12 slices)
1 pint heavy cream
2 oz. dry white wine
salt & pepper to taste
1 Tbsp. finely minced shallots
2 Tbsps. fresh chopped chives

Fold the salmon slices at one end about one third of each slice and then fold into a cone to form a rose shape, 3 each per portion and set aside in the refrigerator.

In a saute pan, reduce the wine and shallots by one half, add the cream and reduce again by one half. Season with salt and pepper and add the chives. Continue to simmer for 3 or 4 minutes.

Pour the sauce onto 4 warm plates, ensuring it is in the center. Roll the sauce around the plate until it covers the plate up to the outer rim. Place the salmon cornets in the center, garnish with a sprig of parsley or dill. Yield: 4 servings.

From: **The Fifth Season**
Marriott City Center Hotel
30 7th Street S.
Minneapolis, Minnesota

Potpourri of Salmon

2 lbs. fresh salmon,
  Norwegian or Alaskan
3 cups heavy cream
salt & pepper to taste
2 oz. white wine or Pernod
2 egg whites
2 Tbsps. chopped fresh
  baby dill or tarragon

Preheat oven to 350 degrees.

Puree fresh salmon in food processor until smooth in texture. Proceed to add cream, a little at a time, and blend gently. Add salt and pepper to taste, wine, egg whites and the fresh dill or tarragon, blending thoroughly. Liberally grease a standard size loaf pan with salad oil and pour salmon mixture into pan. Cover and place in a water bath in oven and bake for 30 minutes. Check for doneness by inserting a toothpick into mousse; if it comes out clean, it's done.

Let rest for a few minutes and then pop mousse out of pan. Serve in ¼" slices hot or chill thoroughly and garnish with fresh watercress sauce, sprig of fresh dill and zest of lemon. Yield: 12 servings.

Watercress Sauce

1 bunch fresh watercress,
  trim leaves, discard stems
2 cups heavy cream
1 Tbsp. chopped shallots
2 ozs. dry white wine
1 oz. each soft butter &
  flour, combined
salt & pepper to taste

Place cream, wine and shallots in a saucepan and put on a slow fire. Reduce by half the original volume. Add flour-butter paste and whip vigorously, until sauce is smooth. Simmer gently for 5 minutes and season. Add fresh watercress and blend thoroughly.

Serve hot with hot salmon mousse as an appetizer or serve chilled with cold mousse as a light luncheon. Yield: 12 servings.

From: **L'Etoile Restaurant**
The St. Paul Hotel
350 Market Street
St. Paul, Minnesota

Smoked Trout Mousse

2 smoked trout, 8 oz. each
4 oz. cream cheese
1½ Tbsps. fresh lemon juice
tabasco sauce to taste
¼ cup chopped onion
whole tomatoes,
    cut thinly into wheels

Remove all skin and bones from one trout. Put trout into food processor, add cream cheese, onion, lemon juice and tabasco sauce. Process until smooth puree has formed.

For an impressive presentation, take the whole trout that is left. Set it on a serving tray on a bed of lettuce leaves. Place whole tomatoes, cut into wedged wheels, around the fish. Put the puree on the tomatoes, garnish with parsley, lemon wedges and cherry tomatoes.

From: **The Trout Haus**
14536 West Freeway Drive
Forest Lake, Minnesota

Soups

Soups

Soup is something that can be a whole meal in itself or it can be the delicately seasoned and appetizing precursor to the entree that follows. The dictionary defines soup as "a liquid food made by cooking meat, vegetables, etc. in water, milk, etc." Technically correct, but how terribly inadequate a description that is. To anyone who has ever eaten a good soup that description leaves everything to the imagination. It certainly wouldn't tempt me if I had never tasted soup before.

Soup is a food that is almost universal, appearing in all the world's memorable cuisines. Every country has its soups, many the mainstay of the general population. Soups are also an opportunity for a chef to exercise his or her talents in the blending of flavors and textures to create something unusual and palate pleasing. Here, then, are some of both from Minnesota's creative chefs.

Afghan Cucumber Soup

3 cups maust
 (yoghurt, plain)
1½ cups chopped cucumber
½ cup seedless raisins,
 (optional)
1 cup cold water
1 Tbsp. fresh dill, chopped
3 Tbsps. chopped chives
½ tsp. salt
2 hard boiled eggs

Beat yoghurt with an electric mixer or with a rotary beater. Add cucumber and the raisins. Add cold water, dill, chives and salt. If the soup is to be mainstay of the meal, add the hard boiled eggs, chopped. Yield: 6 servings.

From: **Caravan Serai**
               2046 Pinehurst Avenue
               St. Paul, Minnesota

Bell Cheese Soup

4 carrots, cut into
  1" matchstick lengths
3 celery ribs, cut into
  1" matchstick lengths
1½ cups chicken stock
2 Tbsps. butter
2 Tbsps. onion, finely chopped
¼ cup flour
3 cups hot chicken stock
1 cup sharp Cheddar cheese
  grated
1 (8.75 oz. can) whole tomatoes,
  chopped (reserve juice)
10 drops of hot pepper sauce
⅛ tsp. nutmeg
salt & pepper to taste
½ cup dry white wine
  (optional)
1½ cups whipping cream,
  heated

Popcorn or chopped chives
  for garnish.

Put carrots and celery in 2-quart saucepan with 1½ cups chicken stock and bring to a boil. Reduce heat and simmer until vegetables are tender. Set aside.

Melt butter in 4- or 5-quart saucepan over medium heat. Add onions and saute until transparent. Do not brown. Add flour, blend well and cook 5-7 minutes, stirring continually; do not cause the roux to brown. Slowly stir in 3 cups hot chicken stock into the flour mixture. Cook over a low heat, stirring continually. Sauce will thicken. Blend in cheese and stir until cheese is melted. Season with hot pepper sauce, nutmeg, wine, salt and pepper. Blend in tomatoes and the vegetables from step 1. Just before serving, add hot cream. Blend well.

Garnish with popcorn or chopped chives.

From: **Jax's Cafe**
University & 20th Ave, N.E.
Minneapolis Minnesota

Bisque de Homard

4 lbs. lobster shells*
6 oz. carrots, chopped
6 oz. onions, chopped
2 oz. celery, chopped
1 clove garlic, crushed
1 tsp. tarragon
1 tsp. thyme
dash of salt, pepper
   and cayenne
2 fresh tomatoes
1 cup + 1 Tbsp. flour
1 gallon water
1 lb. fish bones
bouquet garni (leek, bay leaf,
   parsley tied together)**
9 oz. tomato paste
6 oz. brandy

Heat 4 tablespoons of oil in a large, heavy pot. Saute the lobster shells, crushing them very well. Add salt & pepper, diced carrots, onions, celery, garlic, tarragon and thyme. Cook for 10 minutes over medium heat.

Add the flour. Stir very well.

Add the water and the fish bones, bouquet garni, tomato paste. brandy, cayenne pepper and fresh tomato.

Bring to a boil and simmer for 1 hour.

Strain through a fine china cap and reduce bisque by ⅓. *Serve.*

*When you cook shellfish of any kind—lobster, shrimp, or crayfish, the shells should always be saved, frozen for making stocks and soups such as this one. The shells have more flavor than any other part of the fish.

**Bouquet garni is usually tied up in a small cheesecloth bag which makes for easy removal. In this case cut up the leek and parsley first.

From: **Chez Colette**
L'Hotel Sofitel
5601 West 78th Street
Bloomington, Minnesota

Fennel Cream Soup

½ medium onion, diced
4 slices bacon, diced
2 Tbsps. butter
¼ cup diced carrot
2 lbs. fennel bulb,
  medium diced
12 whole black pepper
  corns
3 bay leaves
1½ qts. rich chicken stock
1 pt. heavy cream
kosher salt
1 stick unsalted butter
1 clove garlic, minced
3 Tbsps. parsley

Saute the onion and bacon in 2 table-spoons of butter over a moderate heat. Add the carrots and fennel and continue cooking until the onions are transparent and the carrots slightly soft. Add bay leaves and pepper-corns, cook another 3 minutes. Add the chicken stock and reduce about half of liquid. Add cream and reduce slightly. While mixture is still warm, place in blender and puree smooth. Strain with fine mesh strainer into large saucepan. Season with salt and a little white pepper. To finish make a garlic compound butter.

Garlic Compound Butter

Place 1 stick of softened, unsalted butter in mixing bowl and whip, with electric mixer until light and fluffy. Add garlic and parsley.

Ladle hot soup into individual soup bowls and spoon a little compound butter on top.

Optional: For a more vibrant green color I suggest adding a few raw spinach leaves to the soup mixture as you puree it in the blender. Add until you get the shade of green that you like. This will not change the flavor significantly.

From:

The 510
510 Groveland Avenue
Minneapolis, Minnesota

Mediterranean Chicken Soup

6 cups rich chicken stock
3-4 Tbsps. pesto,
    without cheese or nuts*
6 oz. tomato paste

1 cup cooked, diced chicken
4-6 oz. homemade
    tarragon fettucini

Julienne of seasonal vegetable
    —zucchini, carrot

*Pesto without cheese or nuts—
2 cups fresh basil leaves; 2 cloves
garlic, slightly mashed; ½ cup olive
oil. Place all in blender and puree.

Add the tomato paste and pesto to the chicken stock, being careful to balance the flavors, so no one predominates.

Add the cooked chicken and noodles, simmer 15-20 minutes. Add the seasonal vegetable and simmer just long enough for vegetable to become slightly tender. Serve.

From: **Treats, Ltd.**
          The Archer House
          212 Division Street
          Northfield, Minnesota

Les Halles
French Onion Soup

4½ cups onions
   finely chopped
3 Tbsps. butter
12 cups water
1 oz. beef bouillon
½ oz. chicken bouillon
½ oz. Kitchen Bouquet
¼ tsp. white pepper
½ tsp. nutmeg
dash Tabasco
dash Hungarian paprika
2 1-oz. slices Provolone
1 1-oz. slice Swiss cheese
2 oz. grated Cheddar cheese

1" thick slices of toasted
   French bread

Melt butter in large skillet. Add onions and cook, stirring until brown. Mix the spices into the onions.

In a large stockpot bring the water to a boil and add bouillons. Stir in the onion mixture and simmer for 30 minutes, stirring occasionally.

In individual ovenproof soup bowls, put soup. Sprinkle with nutmeg, put in slice of toasted French bread, a slice of Provolone, another sprinkle of nutmeg. Add another slice of Provolone, grated Cheddar and a slice of Swiss cheese. Put under broiler until cheese is melted. Serve at once.

From: **Dudley Rigg's
Cafe Espresso**
1430 Washington Avenue S.E.
Minneapolis, Minnesota

Saffron Mussel Soup

24 mussels, washed
  & debearded
1 cup sweet white wine
1 Tbsp. saffron
2 pints of heavy cream
salt & pepper

Beurre Manie:
3 oz. sweet butter, softened
2 oz. flour

Place the mussels in a large saucepan and cover with the white wine. Steam the mussels for 2 or 3 minutes ensuring there is a lid on the pan, until they open. Remove the mussels and discard the shells, leaving the mussels in the wine.

Combine the sweet butter and flour in the beurre manie.

Add the saffron and simmer gently until the saffron has turned the liquor orange in color.

Add the cream and bring to boil, being careful not to burn the cream. Pull the saucepan off the heat and gently whisk in the beurre manie until the soup starts to thicken, season with salt & pepper. Garnish with a fleuron made from puff pastry. Yield: 6 servings.

From: **The Fifth Season**
Marriott City Center Hotel
30 7th Street S.
Minneapolis, Minnesota

Sugar Snap Pea Cream Soup

½ cup chopped leeks
  white parts only
½ cup carrot, diced
½ cup celery, diced
½ cup mushrooms, diced
3 bay leaves
12 whole black peppercorns
1½ qts. rich chicken stock
1 pt. heavy cream
kosher salt
cayenne pepper
2 lbs. sugar snap peas
  stems removed
3 Tbsps. unsalted butter
chervil sprigs

Saute leeks, carrots, celery and mushrooms in butter until carrots are slightly soft. Add bay leaves and peppercorns and cook for 3-5 minutes. Add the chicken stock and reduce one third, then add the cream and reduce it slightly. As the cream and stock mixture reduces, bring 2 quarts of water to a rapid boil and add 1 tablespoon of kosher salt or 2 of regular salt. Add the sugar snap peas to the water and blanch for 1 minute. Remove and rinse in cold water as quickly as possible. The peas should be a bright green color. Take the stock and cream mixture and place in blender, filling about halfway up the container. Add ¼-½ of the blanched peas and puree until smooth. Strain and repeat the process until all of the soup mixture and peas have been used. Take the strained soup mixture and reheat. DO NOT BOIL. Finish with salt and cayenne pepper to taste. Serve in individual bowls and garnish with fresh chervil sprigs. Yield: 6 servings.

From: **The 510**
510 Groveland Avenue
Minneapolis, Minnesota

Cream of Wild Rice Soup

½ cup raw wild rice
5 cups chicken stock

3 ribs celery
2 large carrots
1 large onion
2 Tbsps. butter

5 Tbsps. butter
4 Tbsps. flour

1 cup mushrooms, sliced
½ cup sherry
1 tsp. lemon juice

2 ½ cups half & half
¼ tsp. white pepper
½ tsp. salt

2 slices very crisp bacon

Simmer wild rice in chicken stock until rice is soft. Strain and set rice aside.

Chop celery, onion, and carrots into ¼" dice. Saute the carrots in the butter for 4 minutes. Drain.

In a 3-quart saucepan make the roux using the butter and flour. Cook, stirring occasionally for 4-6 minutes. Add chicken stock, whip to smooth, simmer 5 minutes. If lumpy, strain.

Add vegetables and rice, simmer 15 minutes, stirring frequently.

Simmer the mushrooms for five minutes, add lemon juice and sherry. Add to the soup. Reduce the half and half by half and add to the soup. Season with the salt and pepper. Before serving, crumble a half slice bacon over each bowl. Yield: approximately 32 ounces or 4 servings.

From: Jax Cafe
University & 20th Avenue, N.E.
Minneapolis, Minnesota

Wild Rice Soup

½ lb. bacon, diced
1 cup celery, diced
1 cup onion, diced
1 cup mushrooms, diced

1 can cream mushroom soup
1 can cream celery soup
1½ soup cans water
2 chicken bouillon cubes
1½ cups cooked wild rice
2 pints heavy cream
2 Tbsps. Parmesan cheese
1 Tbsp. soy sauce
pepper to taste

Saute the bacon, celery, onion and mushrooms together.

Put all the other ingredients in the top of large double boiler and add the sauteed vegetables. Cook over medium low heat for two hours in the top of the double boiler before serving. Yield: approximately 32 ounces or ½ gallon.

From: **The Pirate's Cove**
7215 N.E. River Road
Sauk Rapids, Minnesota

Zuppa di Pane con Salcicce

¼ lb. unsalted butter
1 medium white onion, diced
2 quarts chicken stock
1 lb. loaf French bread
    dried
12 oz. Italian sausage, cooked
2 Tbsps. fresh basil
2 Tbsps. fresh oregano
salt to taste
white pepper to taste

In soup kettle melt butter. Add onions and saute until translucent, add the garlic and saute for another 30 seconds. Drain off butter and discard.

Add chicken stock to onions/garlic, bring liquid to a boil and immediately reduce to a simmer.

Add bread, dried and diced into ½" cubes. Simmer, stirring often. Simmer until bread has disintegrated. Add more bread if a thick soup is desired.

Add cooked, drained, chopped Italian sausage. Add fresh herbs. Simmer a few moments. Stir.

Add salt and white pepper to taste.
Serve hot, garnish with fresh herbs.

From: **Figlio's**
            3001 Hennepin Avenue
            Minneapolis, Minnesota

50

SOUPS

Meat & Poultry

Meat & Poultry

Meat and poultry as a food category has probably changed as much as any other single category of food. The interest in health has prompted some people to switch their allegiance to poultry and fish and away from the old mainstays of beef and pork.

Others remain loyal and come up with new and imaginative ways to cook these meats. Veal and lamb are coming into their own in mainstream American cooking. There are recipes here that are variations on classical themes and there are new ways of cooking, saucing and spicing our old favorites. There are some simple, but very tasty recipes like the Pheasant in Sour Cream Sauce for the new or inexperienced, and there are some more elaborate ones like the Lamb Loin in Puff Pastry for those who wish to wow a dinner party.

Italian Meats and Cheeses

One of the cuisines currently much in favor is Italian. For many of us that means a whole new range of cheeses, meats and other victuals with which we're not familiar. One of the restaurants contributing to this book was kind enough to furnish the following guide to Italian meats and cheeses.

Prosciutto is an air-cured meat made from legs of pork. A specialty of the Emilia-Romagna region, the most delicious are produced in and around the town of Parma. The climate of the region gives the Parma hams an unmistakably sweet flavor. Imported Prosciutto had been unavailable in the United States for some time and was not available until March of 1987.

Mortadella is a specialty sausage of Bologna, the capital of the Emilia-Romagna region. Mortadella is the most famous of the Italian sausages. The best Mortadella is made from pork, but there are many varieties, some containing beef and occasionally variety meats. With a diameter of six to eight inches, it is the largest of the Italian sausages.

Pancetta is the closest thing to bacon. Pancetta is salted and rolled pork belly. It is very flavorful and is used as a foundation for many Italian soups and sauces.

Salami is a generally coarse sausage that is produced in every region of Italy. It is usually made from pork and is highly seasoned. The most popular variety is the Genoa salami, and is readily available in the United States.

Capacola-Coppa are meats similar to the Prosciutto ham. They are air-cured, but they come from the shoulder. They are as expensive as Prosciutto and some connoisseurs prefer them. They are highly seasoned, often with hot spices.

Bel Paese literally means beautiful country. It is produced in the region of Lombardy. It is a soft and somewhat mild cheese. It is equally good as a table cheese or in cooking.

Mozzarella is a popular cheese, traditionally made

with buffalo milk, now made with cows' milk. It is made fresh and eaten as soon as possible. Shelf life is about a week, and then it becomes suitable for cooking purposes. Mozzarella can be used in many different ways, deep-fried, baked, and as a topping for pizza.

Gorgonzola is a blue veined, mild cheese, originally produced in caves in the town of the same name, in the region of Lombardy. Most of the Gorgonzola available in the U.S. is called "Dolce Latte," which means it is made with sweet milk. An excellent table cheese, it works equally well in cooking and is very good in a pasta sauce.

Fontina is a semi-hard cheese from the region of Val d'Aosta. It is one of the most famous Italian cheeses. Although it is a table cheese, many great dishes are made with Fontina.

Parmigiano Reggiano is the most famous of all Italian cheeses, is produced all over central and northern Italy. It is in the family of "grana" cheeses, which is a collective term that relates to all hard and mature cheeses. Parmigiano takes at least two years to mature, and the flavor of a good Parmigiano will continue to improve with age. It is versatile and is a good table cheese, is melted in sauces and should be served *freshly grated* over pasta and rice dishes.

In this book Parmigiano cheese is spelled Parmesan because that's the spelling most Americans are familiar with. PLEASE buy it whole and grate it as you use it. The stuff you buy in cans is tasteless, and will definitely affect the results of the recipes you're trying. If you get a piece with rind, cut the rind off carefully and use it in cooking minestrone or other soups. Wonderful!

Beef Curry

1 lb. stew beef
2 onions, chopped
1 Tbsp. flour
1 Tbsp. tomato puree
2 Tbsps. curry powder
1 tsp. salt
pinch pepper
½ tsp. fresh lemon juice
2 cups boiling water
1 beef bouillon cube

Cut the meat into ½" cubes. Brown with the onions in cooking oil. Add the flour, tomato puree, curry powder, salt, pepper, lemon juice and boiling water in which the bouillon cube had been dissolved.

Bring to a boil and then lower heat to a simmer. Simmer for 1½ hours. Serve with boiled rice. Yield: 4-6 generous servings.

*Note—if hotter curry is desired, add 1 tsp. cayenne pepper.

From: **Caravan Serai**
2046 Pinehurst Avenue
St. Paul, Minnesota

Beef Tips in Wild Rice

4 lbs. beef sirloin, cubed
½ cup grated onion
½ cup Burgundy
½ cup Worcestershire sauce
1 Tbsp. Kitchen Bouquet
2 Tbsps. garlic granules
1 Tbsp. paprika
3 Tbsps. beef base
1 Tbsp. black pepper
4 bay leaves

Braise sirloin on grill or under broiler. Place meat in stock pot and add water to just cover beef. Place on heat and add the rest of the ingredients. Bring to a boil and then reduce heat, allowing beef to simmer until tender. Thicken to desired consistency after removing the bay leaves. Serve with wild rice.

From: **The Hubbel House**
SH 57
Mantorville, Minnesota

Madras Beef Curry

2 onions, chopped
6 Tbsps. vegetable oil
2-3 lbs. beef sirloin or chuck,
    cut into 1½" cubes
2 cloves garlic, chopped finely
1 Tbsp. garam masala*
¼ tsp. cayenne
1 large can tomato paste
1 cup water
lemon juice, a good squeeze
salt & pepper to taste

Saute onions in oil until transparent. Add garlic and beef. Cook, stirring, until lightly browned. Make a space in the corner of the skillet and tip to make a pool of oil. Stir in garam masala and cayenne. Cook gently for 30 seconds. Then stir into meat and onions. Add tomato paste, 2 bay leaves and water to make a fairly thin sauce, but not too watery. Add salt and pepper. Cover and cook slowly for about 1 hour. This can be made the day before. It improves with age, gently reheated,

*Note: this is available at Oriental specialty stores or make your own by roasting equal amounts of cardamon seeds, cumin seeds, whole cloves, cinnamon sticks, peppercorns, and coriander seeds at 400 degrees for 20 minutes on a baking sheet. Grind, cover and refrigerate. Keeps up to 6 months.

making sure not to burn. Yield: 6 servings.

From: **Treats, Ltd.**
The Archer House
212 Division Street
Northfield, Minnesota

Pepper Steak

1 8-oz. sirloin steak

cracked pepper
kosher salt
garlic salt
seasoning salt
ground black pepper
¼ lb. butter
¼ cup fresh lemon juice
⅓ cup dry white wine

Press coarsely ground black pepper into both sides of a 2″ thick steak. Sprinkle both sides with kosher salt, garlic salt, seasoning salt and ground black pepper.

In a heavy skillet, melt ¼ cup butter over hot fire, add ¼ cup lemon juice and sear steak on both sides and cook until desired degree of doneness. Transfer meat to serving platter. Heat white wine in skillet with beef juices. Swirl the pan over the flame and pour the juices over the steak.

From: **Michael's Restaurant**
15 South Broadway
Rochester, Minnesota

Roast Tenderloin of Beef
with Five Peppercorns
and Dijon Hollandaise

24 oz. beef tenderloin roast
2 Tbsps. Dijon mustard
½ tsp. each green, black
   white & pink peppercorns,
   chopped
whole cloves
½ cup butter
2 Tbsps. fresh lemon juice
3 egg yolks
2 Tbsps. hot water
2 tsps. Dijon mustard
¼-½ tsp. salt
pinch cayenne pepper

Split the tenderloin ¾ of the way through and lightly salt. Spread the 2 tablespoons of Dijon mustard on the inside. Mix the peppercorns and cloves together and spread onto the mustard.

Truss tenderloin and bake in a preheated oven at 350 degrees for 30-35 minutes for medium rare.

Melt the butter slowly and keep warm. Warm the lemon juice slightly. In the top of double boiler whisk the egg yolks with the lemon juice over simmering water until thick. Whisk in hot water. Whisk thoroughly, adding butter VERY slowly. When butter is all absorbed add the Dijon mustard and the salt and cayenne pepper.

Slice the tenderloin, arrange on platter, or service plates, top with sauce, serve immediately. Yield: 4 servings.

From: **Jax Cafe**
University & 20th Avenue, N.E.
Minneapolis, Minnesota

Loin of Lamb in Puff Pastry

1½ lbs. boneless lamb loin
  (have butcher bone out
  a lamb rack)

1 lb. fresh spinach,
  thoroughly cleaned & drained
1 tsp. fresh garlic
6 paper thin slices of
  prosciutto ham
1 8"x14" sheet puff pastry*
½ cup sliced fresh mushrooms
salt & pepper to taste

*Note—the best puff pastry recipe
is in "The Joy of Cooking."

In a saute pan, saute the garlic with a little butter until translucent. Add spinach and cook quickly until it just begins to wilt. Season with salt and pepper and place in a colander to drain. Set aside.

In another saute pan in a very small amount of butter, saute the lamb loin, fat side first, until brown on all sides. Season lightly and set aside.

Lay out puff pastry sheet and arrange sliced mushrooms down the center for the same length as the lamb loin; layer the ham over the mushrooms; then arrange the spinach to cover the ham evenly. Place lamb loin in the center. Top with remaining ham and spinach, pull up both sides of the puff pastry sheet to completely enclose the lamb. Seal with an egg wash made with a beaten egg and 2 tablespoons of water and invert the completed product on a lightly greased baking sheet. Egg wash the entire surface and make two small slits in top of pastry to allow steam to escape. Bake in a 350-degree oven approximately 30-40 minutes until pastry is golden brown.

Cut off ends of pastry and discard. Slice into 4 even slices and serve with a vin blanc sauce. (A vin blanc sauce is a basic white sauce to which you add dry white wine.) Yield: 4 servings.

From: **L'Etoile Restaurant**
          The St. Paul Hotel
          350 Market Street
          St. Paul, Minnesota

Lamb Chops Raymond

12 lamb chops

2 cups olive oil
½ cup vin rose
1 Tbsp. fresh rosemary,
  finely minced
1 Tbsp. fresh oregano,
  finely minced
1 Tbsp. fresh coriander,
  finely minced
1 Tbsp. fresh parsley,
  finely minced
½ Tbsp. cracked black pepper

4 cups good fresh bread crumbs

Mix together oil, wine and herbs. Marinate the lamb chops for 3 hours in mixture.

Strain the solids from the marinade and add 1½ cups of the marinade liquid to the bread crumbs, tossing lightly until all the liquid is absorbed by the crumbs. Press breading firmly onto chops and refrigerate for ½-1 hour or until breading is set. Heat ½ cup olive oil in a saute pan. Saute chops until golden brown, about 2-3 minutes on a side for medium rare. Then bake in a preheated oven at 350 degrees for 5-8 minutes. Serve with carmelized pearl onions. Yield: 4 servings.

From: **Jax Cafe**
University & 20th Avenue. N.E.
Minneapolis, Minnesota

Layered Pork Loin with Fruit

1 6-8 lb. boneless pork loin,
  well trimmed

Work with your butcher—you need the nicest, lean muscles of the loin. This weight would be about half a whole loin. I ask that the tenderloin be tied in, so I get "light" and "dark" meat. Cross cuts with the fruit stuffing are more delightful looking servings with the 3 colors and textures.

½ lb. dry, pitted prunes
¼ lb. dry apricot halves
½ lb. dry white figs
½ lb. dry black figs
2 Tbsps. dry ginger,
  more if you love it as I do
½ cup candied ginger,
  large pieces
soy sauce
coarse cracked black pepper
1 can crushed pineapple
  (optional)

Gently open the roast without disturbing the butcher's work in rolling the roast. Insert as much dried fruit as you would like, poking it into any cavity in order to produce a cooked slice that is stuffed with fruit. Poke in candied and dry ginger and pour soy sauce in last. Resettle the roast, rub with more ginger and black pepper and cover the top with crushed pineapple, letting juice pool in the baking pan. Take unused dry fruits and soak in water to cover, heat to speed the plumping process, but don't boil. Add sugar to taste and Triple Sec liqueur if desired.

Bake the roast in a preheated 275-degree oven until the meat thermometer registers 175 degrees. Do NOT cook to more than 175 degrees. Overdone pork is ruined pork. Figure about half an hour per pound but use a meat thermometer.

Let the roast stand at least 15 minutes before trying to slice. Do ¾" or less cross cut slices. Serve garnished with plumped fruit and grapes. If you have oranges or other fresh fruit, add them to the platter. This is a fragrant, sensuous entree. We serve it often with creamed whole small red potatoes, generously flavored with dill weed, garnished with sprays of dill weed from our garden.

From: **Mrs. B's Historic Lanesboro Inn**
101 Parkway
Lanesboro, Minnesota

Pork Medallions in Mushroom Beer Gravy

8 pork chops ½" thick,
  remove bone

flour
2 Tbsps. butter
½ cup chopped green onions
2 garlic cloves, minced
1 cup sliced fresh mushrooms
½ tsp. thyme
1 cup beer,
  more if necessary to cover
salt & pepper
minced parsley to garnish

Dust chops until covered with flour. Heat butter in large iron skillet until foaming. Add chops and brown well on both sides. Remove chops and set aside. Add onions and garlic to skillet and saute 2 minutes. Add mushrooms and thyme and saute an additional 3 minutes. Return chops to skillet, add beer and bring to a boil, reduce heat, cover and simmer 1 hour. Transfer chops to serving platter, keep warm. Skim fat from sauce, season with salt and pepper. Spoon sauce over chops and sprinkle with parsley.

From: **The Palmer House**
          500 Sinclair Lewis Avenue
          Sauk Centre, Minnesota

Involtini di Vitello alla Genovese

4 fresh veal cutlets or veal flank,
  pounded thin

2 cups fresh basil, finely chopped
½ cup freshly grated
  Parmesan cheese
½ cup Pignolia nuts
2 cloves garlic
4 oz. olive oil
salt & white pepper to taste

Sprinkle thinly pounded veal with a little salt and white pepper.

Make the pesto by combining all the ingredients in a food processor or blender and blending until smooth. Rub a layer of pesto on the veal and roll up like a pinwheel. Secure with two toothpicks. Dredge veal in flour and saute lightly on all sides. Remove oil and deglaze pan with small amount of cooking alcohol or wine. Serve with sauce.

From: **Pronto Ristorante**
Hyatt Regency Hotel
Minneapolis, Minnesota

Veal Wellington
with Capacola & Spinach

1 6-oz. veal tenderloin

½ oz. fresh spinach,
  wilted in warm butter
2 thin slices Capacola ham
2 oz. Brie cheese
sprig of fresh thyme, chopped
sprig of fresh marjoram, chopped
*1 1" x 5" square puff pastry**

*Note—the best puff pastry recipe is available in "The Joy of Cooking" cookbook.

Brown veal in 2 tablespoons of butter in a very hot pan approximately half a minute on each side, remove from the pan and allow to cool.

Season the cooled veal with a little salt & pepper and the chopped herbs. Place the veal on top of one slice of ham and place the second slice on top of the veal. Fold and tuck the ham around the veal, set to one side.

Place the square of puff pastry on a lightly floured surface and eggwash the outer edges with a wash made of 1 egg beaten with ¼ cup water, about ½" all the way around.

Place the Brie cheese in the center and the spinach leaves over it, place the veal on the spinach, and fold each of the corners of puff pastry towards the other, cutting any excess off with a knife.

Turn the Wellington over and place in a lightly buttered baking pan. Eggwash the pastry to enable it to brown when cooking. Also, a puff pastry braid can be placed over the center for a more attractive appearance. Bake in a preheated 350-degree oven for approximately 20-25 minutes. I recommend a light Madeira sauce to accompany this dish. Yield: 1 serving.

From: **The Fifth Season**
Marriott City Center Hotel
30 7th Street S.
Minneapolis, Minnesota

Champagne Chicken Breasts

6 boneless chicken breasts,
  6-8 oz. each
1 cup seasoned flour*
½ cup melted butter
2 cups champagne

*Seasoned flour—1 cup flour mixed with 2 tablespoons seasoning salt, which Clyde's makes with ½ cup celery salt, ½ cup onion salt, ½ cup garlic salt, ¼ cup garlic powder, 1 tablespoon of thyme, and ¼ cup paprika.

Lightly bread the chicken breasts in the seasoned flour. In a heavy skillet containing the melted butter, lightly brown the chicken breasts on each side. After browning pour off any excess butter.

Add the champagne and simmer the chicken breasts over low heat until tender and the champagne has been reduced to a light glaze. Yield: 6 servings.

From: **Clyde's on the
St. Croix**
Bayport, Minnesota

Chicken Curry

6 onions, peeled, sliced
 and pureed
2 pts. tomato puree
1 Tbsp. coriander
1 Tbsp. cumin
1¼ tsps. turmeric
2½ tsps. cinnamon
½ tsp. ground cloves
1½ tsps. garlic powder
½ tsp. ground ginger
¾ tsp. cayenne pepper
2 qts. chicken stock
2 lbs. chicken strips

Cook onions until golden brown and juices are cooked off. Add tomato puree and spices. Mix well, add chicken stock and simmer one hour.

Add chicken strips and cook until done. Serve over rice pilaf. Yield: 10-12 servings.

From: **Trumpets**
          Butler Square
        100 North Sixth Street
       Minneapolis, Minnesota

Chicken Pauline

1 chicken cut in 8 pieces

onions, chopped
2 Tbsps. minced parsley
½ cup melted butter
½ cup Sauterne

Sprinkle the bottom of a baking dish with onions. Place chicken on onions. Mix the melted butter, minced parsley and Sauterne and pour over the chicken. Bake in a preheated 350-degree oven for 1 hour or until golden brown and cooked through.

From: **The Palmer House**
        500 Sinclair Lewis Avenue
          Sauk Centre, Minnesota

Punjabi Chicken

3 Tbsps. tomato sauce
3 Tbsps. yogurt
4 cloves garlic, chopped
1 1" cube fresh ginger root
  chopped
4 chicken legs & thighs
  cut in half, skin removed
4 whole chicken breasts
  cut in ½, skin removed
6 Tbsps. vegetable oil
1 cinnamon stick
2 bay leaves
6 whole cardamon pods
6 whole cloves
2 chilies or ¼ tsp. cayenne
  pepper (optional)
1 tsp. ground turmeric
1 tsp. salt
black pepper to taste
1 Tbsp. fresh lemon juice

In a small bowl combine tomato sauce, yogurt and 1 cup water. Mix well and set aside.

Put chopped garlic and ginger into blender with 1 tablespoon of water and blend into a smooth paste.

Heat oil in a heavy skillet and brown chicken. Remove from skillet and reserve. Put in cinnamon, bay leaves, cardamon, and cloves and cayenne or chilies, if desired. Add the paste from the blender. Add turmeric, stir for 1 minute.

Put chicken pieces back in, add tomato yogurt mixture, salt, pepper and lemon juice. Bring to a boil. Lower heat, cover and simmer for 25-30 minutes, turning chicken every so often. Uncover pot, raise heat and reduce sauce somewhat. Serve with plain rice.

From:

Treats, Ltd.
The Archer House
212 Division Street
Northfield, Minnesota

Chicken a la Seaver

6 chicken breasts,
   skinned and boned
6 artichoke hearts,
   cooked and drained
6 oz. Swiss cheese
1½ cups bread crumbs
½ cup ground pecans
milk
flour

Lay each chicken breast flat. On one side of breast place 1 ounce of Swiss cheese and 1 artichoke heart, sliced. Fold chicken breast and secure with toothpicks.

Dredge breasts in milk, then in flour, then in milk again before dredging in mixture of the bread crumbs and pecans.

Place on baking sheet and bake in a preheated 350-degree oven until golden brown and chicken is cooked through. Serve with a spicy mustard sauce. Yield: 6 servings.

From: **Trumpets**
Butler Square
100 North Sixth Street
Minneapolis, Minnesota

Stuffed Chicken Breast

4 chicken breasts
   skinned and boned
½ cup butter
¼ cup green onion, chopped
1 cup sliced mushrooms
½ cup dry white wine
½ cup heavy cream
½ cup diced, peeled tomato

Flatten chicken breasts by pounding between two sheets of waxed paper. Heat butter till hot but not brown. Saute chicken on both sides until no longer pink, (4-5 minutes on each side). Place thinly sliced ham on top and fold over. Remove from pan and keep warm. In pan drippings saute onion and mushrooms, add tomato and wine, scraping

4 thin slices ham
4 slices Swiss cheese

up brown pieces. Add cream. Heat slowly until cream reduces and cheese melts (3-4 minutes). Sprinkle with fresh chopped parsley. Serve with sauce spooned over chicken. Serve with wild rice.

From: **Kavanaugh's Restaurant**
2300 Kavanaugh Drive, S.W.
Brainerd, Minnesota

Grilled Duck Breast
with Wild Mushrooms
& Green Peppercorns

2 whole ducks, breasts
   removed from carcasses
2 whole carrots, diced
2 ribs celery, rough cut
8 juniper berries
3 leeks, split & washed
2 garlic cloves
2 bay leaves
1 sprig fresh thyme
2 Tbsps. green peppercorns
1½ cups assorted wild
   mushrooms—chanterelles,
   morels, shitakes
2 shallots, minced
1 cup Rhone wine or any
   red wine from Burgundy

Preheat oven to 350 degrees.

Remove the skin from the breasts, carefully avoiding any tearing of the flesh. Take the carcasses and roast them in the oven until nice and brown. Drain the fat while roasting. You may use this fat to saute potatoes or meats if you wish. This fat may be refrigerated for a week and sometimes longer. Once the ducks have been roasted, remove to a very large stockpot. Saute the carrots, celery and leeks in a little of the duck fat and add juniper berries and garlic. Saute a minute longer and add to the stockpot with the thyme and bay leaves. Cover with water and bring to a boil. Skim the surface and simmer for at least 2-3 hours. Skim

*2 sticks unsalted butter,
  melted*
4 tomatoes, chopped
2 splashes Cognac
kosher salt

occasionally. Add the tomatoes for the last hour of cooking. Strain and reduce this liquid by $^2/_3$. Saute half of the shallots and add reduced stock and red wine and reduce until the liquid begins to thicken slightly. Meanwhile, start the charcoal grill. Wait until the coals become white. Lightly oil breasts with olive or vegetable oil. Season with salt and pepper and place on grill. Cook with skin side down for about 4-5 minutes, being careful not to overcook. They should be medium rare to medium. Then remove and place on a plate and put in a lukewarm oven.

To finish the sauce, turn the heat on low and place sauce over it, whisking in unsalted butter a tablespoon at a time until all but about 2 ounces of butter has been used. Add green peppercorns and Cognac. Adjust seasoning. Saute mushrooms and remaining shallots in butter or duck fat. Place mushrooms on bottom of individual plates, thinly slice each breast and fan out mushrooms. Pour sauce over the top of the duck breasts and mushrooms. Serve either some beet-apple puree or sliced beets with a little sugar and lemon to accompany the duck. Yield: 4 servings.

From: **The 510**
510 Groveland Avenue
Minneapolis, Minnesota

Rosy Glazed Goose with Apple Stuffing

¼ cup butter
2 medium onions, chopped
2 ribs celery, chopped
½ cup dry vermouth
12 tart apples
    sliced into 8 pieces each
1½ cups apple juice
1 bag (8 oz.) herb-seasoned
    stuffing mix
1 tsp. salt
¼ tsp. pepper
1 10-12 lb. goose or
    2 4-5 lb. ducks
Rosy Glaze

Melt butter in a large skillet. Add onions and celery and saute until limp, about 3 minutes. Add vermouth and simmer 10 minutes. Add apples and saute 5 minutes. Add apple juice, stuffing mix, salt and pepper, stirring well to combine. Remove from heat and allow to cool for about 10 minutes. Preheat oven to 325 degrees. Stuff cavity of goose with cooled stuffing and skewer closed. Place goose on rack in roasting pan. Cook in oven for 2½-3 hours or until meat thermometer reads 185 degrees. Carefully drain accumulating fat at least twice during cooking, or as necessary. Discard fat. During the last half hour of cooking, baste with Rosy Glaze. Carve goose and arrange on serving platter with stuffing. Serve goose with remaining glaze. Yield: 4-6 servings.

Rosy Glaze

1 cup orange juice
¼ cup lemon juice
½ cup cranberry juice
¾ cup sweet vermouth
1 tsp. mustard
¼ tsp. garlic powder
¼ tsp. onion powder
2 Tbsps. cornstarch
1 10-oz. jar currant jelly

In a small saucepan, combine all the ingredients. Heat over medium heat for 12 minutes or until mixture boils, stirring occasionally. Lower heat and simmer for 15 minutes.

From: **The Anderson House**
333 West Main Street
Wabasha, Minnesota

Pheasant in Sour Cream Sauce

2 pheasants, 1¾ lbs. each
2 cups flour
½ cup cooking oil
salt & pepper

1 cup cream
1 cup milk
2 cups water
2 tsps. chicken base
¼ tsp. white pepper
½ tsp. garlic powder
½ cup sour cream

Roux:
1 oz. flour
1 oz. butter

Cut pheasants in 8 pieces, splitting each breast. Dust cut pieces of pheasant in flour and saute in frying pan with oil, until golden brown. Salt and pepper birds and remove to a roasting pan. Set aside.

To prepare roux, put butter and flour in small, heavy bottomed pan over low heat and cook, stirring, for several minutes. The cooking removes the pasty taste of the flour.

Put cream, milk, and water in saucepan. Add chicken base, pepper, and garlic. Bring mixture to approximately 170 degrees and thicken with roux. Add the sour cream to mixture and stir until dissolved. Pour sauce over pheasants in roasting pan. Cover and bake at 325 degrees for 2 hours or until all the pheasant is tender. Pour off the sour cream sauce and serve with fowl. Wild rice is an excellent accompanying dish with this. Yield: 4 servings.

From: **Michael's Restaurant**
15 South Broadway
Rochester, Minnesota

Fish & Seafood

Fish & Seafood

More and more people are discovering fish and seafood. Chefs are partially responsible for this as they prepare these delicacies in ever more enticing and appetizing ways.

The only drawback to all of this is, of course, the rising price of fish. That, however, may be ameliorated by the new science of aquaculture. Catfish farms were the first and now most restaurants that serve catfish, and indeed, most that is sold through markets is farm catfish. The Scots and the Norwegians have begun farming Atlantic salmon, so there is progress in all directions.

Here you will find some traditional recipes like Beer Batter for the fish fry as well as innovations like Lobster Medallions with Wild Mushrooms. Whatever your taste for fish, there's a way to prepare it here.

Beer Batter for Fish

¼ cup Fitger's Beer
½ tsp. baking soda
1¼ cups sifted flour
1 tsp. sugar
2 Tbsps. shortening
1 tsp. baking powder

Mix the beer and the soda together. Add the remaining ingredients together, beating with a rotary beater until smooth.

After lightly breading walleye or the fish fillets of your choice in flour, seasoned to taste, dip the fish into Fitger's Beer Batter. Deep fry in enough oil to cover the fillets. Cook until golden brown. Yield: Enough batter to do 6-8 fillets.

From: **Fitger's Inn**
600 East Superior Street
Duluth, Minnesota

Lake Superior Fish Cakes

5 lbs. fresh Northern Pike
   or Herring fillets, skin removed
2 small onions, size of egg
¼ cup melted butter
1 tsp. (scant) nutmeg
⅛ tsp. curry powder
4 Tbsps. cornstarch
3 large cans evaporated milk
2 cups whole milk
5 eggs
4 Tbsps. salt

Grind the fish fillets and onion together. Add melted butter, nutmeg, curry powder and cornstarch together.

Mix very thoroughly. Add 1 egg and 1 cup milk, beat very hard. Add remaining eggs. Gradually add milk and salt. Beat until batter is very smooth.

Drop by tablespoonfuls onto a grill or frying pan with enough oil to brown and prevent sticking. Cook on medium heat. Brown both sides evenly. Serve with good tartar sauce.

From: **The East Bay Hotel**
        Grand Marais, Minnesota

Lobster Medallions
with Wild Mushrooms
and Sauce Americaine

You need to begin the Americaine reduction 24 hours in advance.

4 6-8 oz. lobster tails

2 cups basic Beurre Blanc Sauce

2 cups mirepoix (celery, carrot,
   onion, chopped)
1 qt. water
½ pt. brandy
1 pt. fish stock

Remove lobster meat from shells, set meat aside. Place mirepoix and lobster shells in roasting pan and brown in oven. Deglaze roaster with brandy and water on top of stove, being careful to scrape up brown bits. Put all in large stockpot.

Add fish stock, veal demi-glace, tomato paste and spices. Bring to a boil, reduce to a simmer and cook, covered, for 12 hours.

1 pt. veal demi-glace*
½ cup tomato paste
2 bay leaves
½ tsp. thyme
½ tsp. shallots, minced
½ tsp. sage

After straining reduce mixture to a thick consistency yielding 1-2 cups of sauce Americaine.

Combine Americaine with Beurre Blanc.

Slice lobster meat crosswise into medallions, saute quickly 1-2 minutes per side in clarified butter**. Place medallions in a pool of Americaine sauce. Top with lightly sauteed wild mushrooms (any seasonal mushroom will do). Yield: 2 servings.

*Demi-glace is simply any meat stock that has been reduced by half to a thick consistency.

**Clarified butter is butter which has been melted and skimmed off, leaving the whey. It is clear yellow.

Beurre Blanc

⅓ cup white wine vinegar
2½ Tbsps. each lemon juice and
    dry white vermouth
1 Tbsp. shallots, finely minced
½ tsp. salt
pinch white pepper
½-¾ lb. butter, chilled,
    cut into ¼" bits

In a large heavy enamel saucepan bring vinegar, lemon juice, vermouth, shallots, salt and pepper to a boil. Cook until liquid has reduced to 2 tablespoons.

Remove the saucepan from the heat and immediately beat in 2 of the bits of butter, using a wire whisk. As the butter softens and begins to blend in with the liquid, add another and keep beating. Place back over very low heat, continuing to add the bits of butter and whisking constantly, as each piece blends into the sauce. Sauce should become thick and creamy colored and the consistency of a light cream sauce or hollandaise. Remove from heat at once and season to taste.

If not used at once, keep warm over barely warm water. Don't reheat directly as sauce will probably separate. Should make 2 cups.

From: **The Blue Horse**
1355 University Avenue
St. Paul, Minnesota

78

Oysters Fitger's

32 fresh oysters

Open the oysters, keeping them on the half shell. Rinse any grit or mud from the oysters or shells.

Sauce:
¼ lb. butter
2 cups half & half
¼ tsp. seasoning salt
¼ tsp. basil
¼ tsp. lemon pepper
¼ tsp. dill weed

¼ cup roasted macadamia nuts
¼ cup artichoke hearts
¼ cup crisp bacon
¼ cup onions
½ cup frozen spinach,
*   thawed and drained*
½ tsp. fresh garlic, minced
⅛ cup capers

Breading:
½ cup fine bread crumbs
½ cup freshly grated
*   Parmesan cheese*
¼ cup minced parsley

Melt the butter, whisk in the cream, herbs, salts and pepper.

Chop finely the nuts, artichoke hearts, bacon, onions and spinach. Add those with garlic and capers to the sauce. Simmer over a low heat for 15-20 minutes.

Prepare the breading, mixing bread crumbs, cheese and parsley together thoroughly.

Top each oyster with the prepared sauce. On top of the sauce, add breading. Set on a sheet pan and bake at 350 degrees for 20-25 minutes or until the sauce bubbles and the breading browns. Yield: 8 servings, 4 oysters each.

From: **Fitger's Inn**
600 East Superior Street
Duluth, Minnesota

Broiled Rainbow Trout

10 8-oz. whole rainbow trout

butter
Bermuda onion, finely chopped
lemon pepper
salt
fresh lemon slices

Wash the trout, cut up backbone from the inside (butterfly). Place trout in broiler, skin side up, at least 4″ from the flame.

Turn the trout meat side up, sprinkle with salt and lemon pepper, adding approximately 3 tsps. butter on surface of each fish. Broil until butter starts to melt.

Add chopped onions, let cook until slightly brown.

Add lemon slices, put under broiler for a minute. It is very important that the fish does not become overcooked. It should be checked constantly, the trout will become white in color and flake easily when tested with a fork. The length of time will vary depending on the thickness of the trout.

From: **The Trout Haus**
14536 West Freeway Drive
Forest Lake, Minnesota

Trout Florentine

6 10-14 oz. fresh rainbow trout

½ lb. bacon
½ cup finely chopped carrots
½ cup finely chopped onions
2 oz. Pernod or Anisette
3 cups heavy cream

Spinach
  18 large leaves, ribs removed
  6 cups leaves, quartered

Dress, butterfly and bone trout. Reserve. Dice or shred the bacon (frozen is easiest). Saute until half done, then add the carrots, cooking for 3 minutes and stirring frequently. Add the onions, cooking for another 3 minutes, then drain the fat.

Put back on the heat and flame with the Pernod or Anisette. Add the cream and reduce by half.

Saute the trout in olive oil and reserve. While the sauce is reducing, dip 18 leaves in sauce, arrange 3 under each trout. When the sauce is done, add ¼ tsp. salt and pinch of pepper. Divide the 6 cups of leaves, which have been tossed, evenly over trout, pour sauce over all and serve immediately with boiled red potatoes. Yield: 6 servings.

From: **Jax Cafe**
University & 20th Avenue, N.E.
Minneapolis, Minnesota

Trout Frangelica

6 10-14 oz. rainbow trout

½ cup hazelnuts
½ cup butter
1 cup Frangelica liqueur

Dress, butterfly and bone trout. Reserve.
Roast, remove skin and finely chop hazelnuts. A food processor works best for this.
Slice butter into 1 tablespoon-size pieces and allow to warm to room temperature.
Dust the trout with flour seasoned to taste and saute in peanut oil.
Heat the Frangelica in saute pan. Flame the liqueur and reduce to a syrup-like consistency. Add butter pieces one at a time while shaking or swirling the pan until melted. Add pinch of salt.
Arrange trout on heated platter or hot service plates. Sprinkle with chopped hazelnuts. Pour sauce over trout, garnish with fresh parsley. Serve immediately.

Grand Marnier Variation

Follow recipe for Frangelica substituting walnuts for hazelnuts and Grand Marnier for Frangelica and grated orange rind for parsley.

From: **Jax Cafe**
University & 20th Avenue, N.E.
Minneapolis, Minnesota

Grilled Salmon
with Raspberry Beurre Blanc Sauce

6 7-oz. fresh salmon steaks
  or fillets, ¾" thick

salad oil
salt & black pepper

½ cup fresh raspberries
2 ozs. raspberry vinegar or
  white vinegar
2 ozs. dry vermouth
1 Tbsp. chopped shallots
2 sticks chilled butter

Preheat gas grill or prepare a hot fire using standard charcoal briquets. Brush salad oil onto salmon steaks liberally and season to your taste. Place steaks on hot grill and cook approximately 4 minutes on each side, giving them a quarter turn on each side as well in order to achieve attractive grill markings. The fish may also be cooked in a broiler in a conventional stove.

Meanwhile, place raspberry vinegar, dry vermouth and chopped shallots in a small saucepan and reduce mixture over medium heat down to a syrup. Proceed to whip in butter, a little at a time, over low heat. When all the butter has been whipped in, the sauce should be slightly thick in texture. Remove from heat and hold in a warm place. Serve with grilled salmon. Yield: 6 servings.

From: **L'Etoile Restaurant**
The St. Paul Hotel
350 Market Street
St. Paul, Minnesota

Grilled Roma Salmon

2 lbs. fresh or frozen salmon

1 cup freshly grated
  Parmesan cheese
½ cup chopped fresh parsley

Marinade:
½ cup olive oil
½ cup white wine
1 tsp. crushed fresh garlic
¼ tsp. salt
¼ tsp. white pepper
¼ cup white vinegar
½ tsp. thyme
¼ tsp. oregano

Marinate salmon, cut into 8-ounce portions, for 1 hour.* Place on grill, 4″ above the coals. This can also be done in the broiler. Cook for approximately 3 minutes. Turn over and top with the Parmesan cheese. Cook until salmon flakes. Remove and garnish with lemon wedges and chopped parsley. Yield: 4 servings.

*Note—It is important that salmon should not be marinated for more than an hour.

From: **Muffuleta in the Park**
2260 Como Avenue
St. Paul, Minnesota

Sole with
Minted Mousseline Sauce

6 7-9 oz. fillets of sole

1 cup butter
1 Tbsp. fresh lime juice
3 egg yolks
2 Tbsps. hot water
½ tsp. grated lime rind
¾ tsp. fresh mint leaves, minced
½ cup heavy cream, whipped

3 limes

Wash fillets and pat dry with paper towels. Fold to approximate even thickness. The fillets will not look quite as nice, but the edges will not dry out. Brush with butter and lightly season with salt and pepper. Butter a pan and put the fillets in the pan.

Melt the butter and reserve ½ cup. Warm the lime juice and whisk the juice with the egg yolks in the top of a double boiler over simmering water. Whisk until mixture begins to thicken. Whisk in the hot water and begin adding the rest of the butter, very slowly. Then add the lime rind, fresh mint leaves, salt and a pinch of cayenne pepper. Fold in the whipped cream. Hold in a warm place.

Peel the limes by cutting skin down to flesh, slice each into 8 very thin slices. Arrange 4 slices on each fillet, slightly overlapping them. Bake in a preheated oven at 350 degrees for 8-10 minutes. Sauce individually on hot service plates or platter. Serve immediately.

From: **Jax Cafe**
University & 20th Avenue, N.E.
Minneapolis, Minnesota

Stuffed Sole

2½ lbs. sole fillets
4 cups rice mix
½ lb. butter
2 dashes Tabasco sauce
¼ cup lemon juice
3 chicken bouillon cubes
8 ozs. sharp Cheddar cheese,
   shredded
4 ozs. Swiss cheese, shredded

Rice Mix:
3 cups cooked white rice
½ cup diced mushrooms
¼ cup diced celery
¼ cup diced pimento
¼ cup diced onion

Mix rice together with mushrooms, celery, pimento, onion and half of cheese. Layer in baking pan with fillets of sole. Melt butter, add lemon and tabasco to chicken bouillon, pour over fish and rice and bake at 350 degrees for approximately 20 minutes. When sole is done, sprinkle the rest of the cheese on top, melt and serve. Yield: 6 servings.

From: **The Pirate's Cove**
7215 N.E. River Road
Sauk Rapids, Minnesota

Vegetables

Vegetables

Vegetables have come full circle. Time was when they were the subject of jokes, of children whining "Do I have to eat this?" Part of the problem with vegetables might have been the way the poor things were treated—often just thrown in a pot and left to boil endlessly until all color and flavor had fled. This has changed and so have the vegetables themselves.

Growers are giving us new and exotic vegetables we have never seen before. White eggplant, peppers in every conceivable color; there is even a potato with a royal purple skin. We have Italian and Oriental vegetables we never knew existed. And we have the current mania, in some cooking circles, for miniature vegetables. On those I tend to agree with Craig Claiborne, the New York Times food critic and cookbook author, who said he is not amused and achieves better results with vegetables of standard measurement.

Minnesota's chefs provide some interesting variations on standard vegetables. With these there should be no more "Do I have to eat this?" at your house.

Barley Casserole

¼ cup butter
1 medium onion, finely chopped
¼ lb. mushrooms, thinly sliced
2 chicken bouillon cubes
1 quart water
1 cup medium sized
   pearled barley
1 tsp. salt

Preheat oven to 350 degrees.

Melt butter in a 10″ skillet over moderately low heat. Add onion and mushrooms and cook, stirring often, until wilted. In a 1½-2-quart saucepan bring bouillon cubes and water to a boil, stirring to dissolve the cubes. Turn barley into a round, ungreased 2-quart casserole, stir in onion-mushroom mixture, the very hot bouillon and salt. Bake, uncovered, in preheated 350-degree oven, stirring several times, for 1 hour. Cover tightly, continue baking until liquid has been absorbed and barley is tender but chewy, about 30 minutes. Serve hot. Yield: 8 servings.

From: **The Anderson House**
333 West Main Street
Wabasha, Minnesota

Broccoli Egg Bake

2 lbs. broccoli, cut in flowerettes
½ cup onions, thinly sliced
¼ cup butter
8 hard boiled eggs
1 cup fresh mushrooms, sliced
1½ cups heavy cream
1 tsp. Dijon mustard
1 tsp. salt
1 tsp. dill weed
1 tsp. white pepper
½ lb. natural Swiss cheese slices
8-10 thin slices cocktail rye bread

Preheat oven to 350 degrees.

Cook broccoli in salted, boiling water until broccoli can be pierced with a fork. Drain and cool down in cold water. Layer in the bottom of a casserole. Saute onions in 1½ table-spoons of butter until softened. Spread over broccoli. Slice hard boiled eggs over onions. Saute mushrooms in the remaining butter for several minutes. Add cream and simmer until cream reduces by ½ cup.

Mix in mustard, salt, dill weed and white pepper. Pour over eggs. Top with cheese slices, overlap bread slices on top of cheese. Bake for 45-50 minutes.

From: **Kavanaugh's Restaurant**
2300 Kavanaugh Drive, S.W.
Brainerd, Minnesota

Sherried Mushrooms

4 cups small fresh
  button mushrooms
½ cup melted butter
½ cup seasoned flour
1 cup sherry

Lightly bread the mushrooms in the seasoned flour. Melt the butter in a frying pan, saute the mushrooms until lightly browned. Add the sherry and simmer over low heat until the sherry reduces to a light glaze over the mushrooms. Yield: 4 servings.

Seasoned Flour:
1 cup all-purpose flour
2 Tbsps. seasoned salt

Mix together throughly.

Seasoned Salt:
½ cup celery salt
½ cup onion salt
½ cup garlic salt
¼ cup garlic powder
1 Tbsp. thyme
¼ cup paprika

Mix ingredients together. Yield: 2 cups.

From: **Clyde's on the
St. Croix**
Bayport, Minnesota

90

Peas and Beet Greens

2 lbs. shelled peas
2 cups chicken stock
¼ tsp. mace
½ tsp. thyme
1 bay leaf, crumbled
⅛ tsp. freshly ground pepper
⅛ tsp. salt
¾ cup baby beet greens,
   rinsed & dried

Heat chicken stock in medium saucepan to boiling. Add peas, mace, thyme, crumbled bay leaf, salt and pepper. Cook, covered for 1 minute. Add beet greens, re-cover and cook 1-2 minutes until greens are slightly wilted. Remove from heat, adjust seasonings and serve immediately in heated bowls.

From: **Mrs. B's Historic Lanesboro Inn**
101 Parkway
Lanesboro, Minnesota

Butter Baked Potatoes

A big favorite!

6 long, white potatoes,
  Kennebecs are good
1 stick butter, melted
salt, pepper, other seasonings to
  suit taste & menu (paprika,
  garlic salt, basil, rosemary,
  dill, cayenne, parsley,
  onion powder, or ?)

Preheat oven to 450 degrees.

Scrub potatoes thoroughly and cut in fourths the long way. Dip in melted butter and place skin side *down* in baking pan. Sprinkle with seasoning—(I always use freshly ground black pepper).

Bake for about 1 hour until brown and tender. These are great with roast beef, ribs, fried chicken, sausages, hamburgers. They may be dipped in hot sauce, sprinkled with bacon bits, melted cheese, salsa, etc.

From: **Mrs. B's Historic
        Lanesboro Inn**
        101 Parkway
        Lanesboro, Minnesota

92

VEGETABLES

Twice Baked Potatoes

4 large baking potatoes

¾ cup sour cream
½ cup green onion, chopped
¼ cup crisp bacon, crumbled
1 tsp. chicken bouillon
1 tsp. ground mustard
½ tsp. white pepper
2 tsps. garlic salt
½ cup Cheddar cheese, grated

Scrub potatoes and bake in a preheated 350-degree oven until done. Remove from oven and cool.

Slice off top of each potato and scoop out insides into a mixing bowl. Add sour cream and all other ingredients except cheese. Mix thoroughly. Put mixture back into the skins, top with grated Cheddar cheese and put under the broiler for 5-10 minutes until brown and crunchy on top. Yield: 4 servings.

From: **The Thayer Hotel**
Hwy. 55
Annandale, Minnesota

Red Cabbage

1 medium head red cabbage
1 medium sweet onion
2 large apples
1 Tbsp. bacon fat
1 tsp. salt
½ cup sugar
1½ cups water
1 cup vinegar

Wash and remove outer leaves of cabbage. Remove core and slice. Peel and slice onion. Peel and quarter apples, removing core. Put all remaining ingredients except the cornstarch in a saucepan. Add cabbage, onion and apples. Cover and simmer for 20 minutes.

Add a small amount of cornstarch to

1 bay leaf
2 whole allspice
2 whole cloves, heads removed
6 peppercorns
cornstarch to thicken

thicken the sauce. Remove bay leaf, whole allspice, cloves. Serve.

From: **The Lowell Inn**
102 North Second Street
Stillwater, Minnesota

Spinach Balls

2 10-oz. pkgs. frozen spinach,
thawed, drained & chopped
2 cups herb stuffing mix
2 onions, finely chopped
½ tsp. thyme
¾ cup melted butter
½ cup freshly grated
Parmesan cheese
6 eggs, beaten
½ Tbsp. black pepper

Preheat oven to 350 degrees.
Mix all ingredients together thoroughly. Form into small balls (marble sized) and bake on a greased cookie sheet for 20 minutes.

From: **The Anderson House**
333 West Main Street
Wabasha, Minnesota

Baked Tomatoes Florentine

6 medium size tomatoes
salt
½ cup light cream
1 egg yolk
12 oz. fresh spinach,
   cooked, drained and chopped
¼ tsp. horseradish
3 Tbsps. melted butter
2 hard cooked eggs, sieved

Preheat oven to 375 degrees.

Cut top off each tomato. Scoop out juice and seeds. Sprinkle insides with salt. Combine the cream and egg yolk; add chopped spinach, horseradish, and 1 tablespoon of butter. Salt to taste. Heat and stir just until it simmers. Fill tomatoes with the creamed spinach. Place in a 10" x 6" baking dish. Top each tomato with melted butter. Bake for 25 minutes. Serve hot with sieved hard boiled eggs sprinkled on top of each. Yield: 6 servings.

From: **The Anderson House**
333 West Main Street
Wabasha, Minnesota

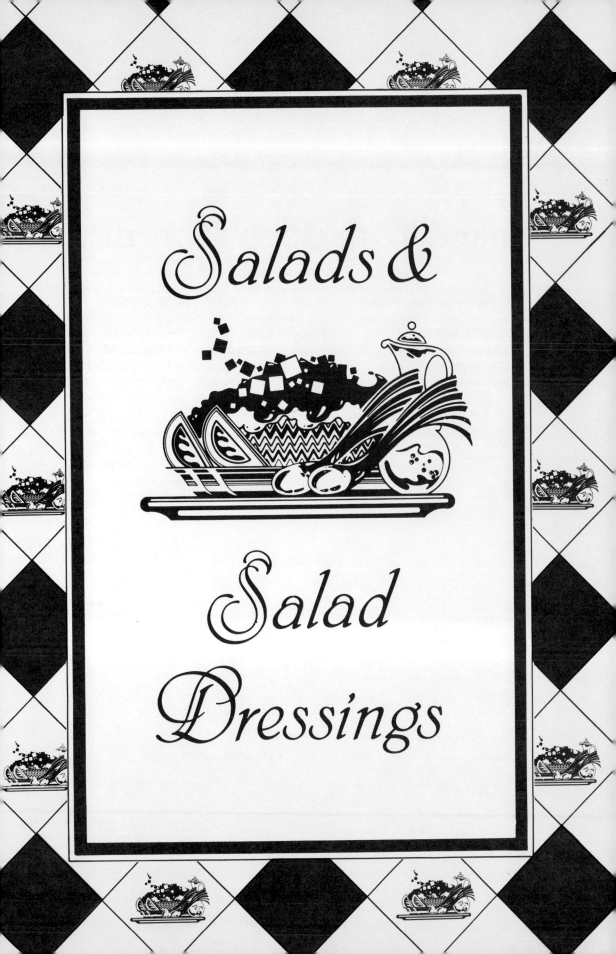

Salads &

Salad
Dressings

Salads & Salad Dressings

Salads have evolved from something that simply accompanies a meal, a course between other more important courses, to wonderful amalgamations of taste and texture. The imagination of Minnesota's chefs comes to the fore with recipes like a Wild Rice and Duck Salad with Chutney Dressing.

Of course, we have some of the old favorites, too, like a Caesar Salad. And variations on classic themes—Oriental Chicken and Tarragon Chicken salads. Dressings, too, show imagination with the use of fresh ginger, curry, and fruit juices. You should be able to find a salad to accompany any meal, to be the meal itself or just to eat in lonely splendour on your own.

There are new dressings, too. Afer all, what is a salad without dressing—naked, uninteresting. As in high fashion, dressing is everything.

Belgian Endive and Strawberry Salad

4 whole Belgian endive
½ pt. strawberries,
   stemmed & sliced
12 mint leaves
1 tsp. chopped parsley
½ cup chopped radicchio
1 Tbsp. chopped pecans
kosher salt to taste
black pepper to taste

Vinaigrette:
½ cup extra virgin olive oil
½ cup walnut oil
1 Tbsp. lemon juice
1 Tbsp. raspberry vinegar
½ tsp. shallots, minced
salt

Make the vinaigrette by combining all ingredients and blending until well mixed, then season with salt. Take endive and slice crosswise into ¼" strips. Add remaining ingredients, except for strawberries and mint, and toss with the vinaigrette. Sprinkle a little sugar on the strawberries, then add to the salad and toss lightly. You do not want the berries to bleed into the endive. Check seasoning by using kosher salt only. Regular salt will wilt the leaves too quickly. Add coarse ground black pepper and serve on chilled plates. Top each salad with 3 leaves of mint, arranged either in the center of the salad, or on the outer edge of the salad. You may want to fan a strawberry or so for further garnish. Also tart blueberries may be substituted for the strawberries. Do not use any frozen fruit for this dish.

From: **The 510**
510 Groveland Avenue
Minneapolis, Minnesota

Caesar Salad

1 head crisp romaine lettuce
1 clove garlic, crushed
½ tsp. freshly ground
   black pepper
juice ½ lemon
1 tsp. Worcestershire sauce
1 small tin anchovies
1 tsp. Dijon mustard
6 Tbsps. imported olive oil
2 Tbsps. French wine vinegar
2 coddled eggs (boiled 1 min.)
2 Tbsps. butter
½ cup croutons
½ cup Parmesan cheese,
   freshly grated

Trim romaine and cut lengthwise twice and then crosswise about 1½" apart. Or tear the romaine into pieces about the same size, if you're a purist. Rub crushed garlic around the bottom of a large wooden bowl. Retain pulp. Add crushed pepper, lemon juice, Worcestershire sauce and anchovies. With a fork, mash anchovies against the bottom of the bowl into a fine paste. Add mustard, olive oil and vinegar; blend thoroughly. In a separate dish beat the coddled eggs, then add them to the above mixture and beat vigorously until dressing begins to thicken. In a shallow frying or crepe pan, melt the butter and saute the garlic pulp. When the garlic pulp begins to be aromatic, add croutons and saute until lightly browned. Place romaine in wooden bowl and toss thoroughly. Add ¼ cup Parmesan cheese and croutons; toss lightly. Serve salad onto well chilled salad plates, topping each portion with Parmesan cheese.

From: **The Blue Horse**
           1355 University Avenue
           St. Paul, Minnesota

Oriental Chicken Salad

chicken stock or water with
   1 chicken bouillon cube,
   dissolved

Begin by poaching chicken breasts in chicken stock. Cool and slice.
Arrange a base of Bibb lettuce on a plate. Arrange a hexagon pattern with Daikon rad-

2 chicken breasts,
  poached and skinned
12 pieces Daikon radish, julienne
12 pieces red bell pepper, julienne
4-6 leaves Bibb lettuce
1 cup steamed Cantonese
  noodles
2 tsps. sauteed, sliced almonds
2 tsps. green onion tops, julienne
12 pieces enoki mushrooms

Dressing:
½-⅓ cup good soy sauce
¼ cup sesame oil
1-2 Tbsps. grated fresh ginger
1 tsp. grated orange rind
½ tsp. five spice*
¼ cup hoisin sauce*

*Note: These may be obtained in
Oriental specialty stores.

ish and red bell pepper. Place noodles, which have also been cooked, in center of plate. Top with chicken breast, apply a generous amount of dressing. Garnish with almonds, onions and mushrooms.

From: **The Blue Horse**
1355 University Avenue
St. Paul, Minnesota

Tarragon Chicken Salad

2½-3 lbs. diced white
  chicken meat, cooked
2 cups diced celery
1 cup mayonnaise, good quality,
  homemade preferably
1 cup sour cream or crème fraîche
3-4 Tbsps. dried tarragon—
  fresh in season
½ cup hazelnuts, chopped

Put chicken and celery in bowl, add mayonnaise and sour cream or crème fraîche. Add tarragon, remembering if using fresh, it will take almost double the amount to achieve the same strength seasoning. Add hazelnuts and serve. Yield: 8-10 servings.

From: **Treats, Ltd.**
The Archer House
212 Division Street
Northfield, Minnesota

Wild Rice and Duck Salad
with Chutney Dressing

Dressing:
*1 cup prepared chutney
  (Major Grey's)*
½ cup honey
¼ cup cider vinegar
½ tsp. ginger
½ tsp. white pepper
½ tsp. dry mustard
½ tsp. salt
½ tsp. curry powder

Salad Ingredients:
3 cups wild rice, cooked & chilled
2 cups cooked duck meat, diced
1 medium green pepper, julienne
1 medium red pepper, julienne
1 red onion, julienne
½ cup sliced water chestnuts
*½ cup fresh pineapple,
  cut in chunks*
*½ cup mandarin oranges,
  drained, chilled & reserved*
*½ cup toasted, slivered almonds,
  reserved*

Combine the ingredients for the dressing in a blender or food processor until smooth.

Combine all the ingredients for the salad, except those to be reserved, and add dressing, mixing well. Add the mandarin oranges and toss lightly. Sprinkle with toasted almonds at time of service.

This salad is beautiful when presented in individual "cups" made of red cabbage leaves. Crusty French bread, scones, or biscuits make good accompaniments. Yield: 6 servings.

From: **Jax Cafe**
University & 20th Avenue, N.E.
Minneapolis, Minnesota

Wild Rice and Smoked Turkey Salad

Wild Rice:
1 cup wild rice, washed
2 Tbsps. butter
1 onion, diced small
2¼ cups chicken broth, hot

Dressing:
1 egg yolk
4 tsps. cream sherry
1 tsp. lemon juice
½ tsp. Dijon mustard
¼ tsp. salt
⅛ tsp. white pepper
1 Tbsp. heavy cream

Salad:
¼ cup minced celery
½ cup minced green onion
1 red onion, julienne
6 oz. red seedless grapes
4 oz. pecan halves
8 oz. smoked breast of turkey

In a saucepan with a lid, saute the wild rice in butter 2-3 minutes. Add the onion and saute until onion is transparent. Add the hot broth and bring to a boil. Reduce heat and cover. Simmer for about 45 minutes or until all the liquid is absorbed. Remove from heat and refrigerate 2-3 hours until chilled. Meanwhile, make the dressing.

Place the egg yolk in a mixing bowl and beat well with a wire whisk. Add the sherry, lemon juice, mustard, salt and pepper and beat well. Continue whipping while adding the oil in a slow steady stream. When all the oil is incorporated, whip in the heavy cream. Refrigerate until ready for use.

When the rice is chilled, mix in the chopped celery and green onions. Arrange on four plates on beds of red leaf lettuce. Top each salad with equal amounts of onions, grapes and pecans. Slice the smoked turkey in long strips ¼" thick. Fan slices out atop the salads and top with dressing. Yield: 4 servings.

From: **W.A. Frost & Company**
374 Selby Avenue
St. Paul, Minnesota

102

102

SALADS & SALAD DRESSINGS

Winter Salad for Minnesota

½ chopped onion
2 cups diced, cooked potatoes
1 cup carrots,
    cut into pretty shapes
1 cup diced celery
3 hardcooked eggs, quartered
3 sweet pickles

Optional:
2 cups cooked meat; ham, turkey,
    chicken, etc.
1 cup green beans, cooked
1 cup kidney beans
1 cup garbanzo beans
1 cup green peas
1 cup chopped, drained tomato
½ cup sliced new leeks

Green onions, olives, parsley, green and red pepper are all good additions. This is a good salad to prepare ahead. Best dressed and "cured" overnight—24 hours in the refrigerator. Use boiled dressing or your favorite Italian style. This is very similar to many northern European, French and Russian recipes. Any cold weather culture has its own version.

Boiled Dressing:
3 eggs, beaten
½ cup vinegar
½ cup water
1 cup sugar, less if you prefer
salt, pepper, cumin to taste
1 Tbsp. flour
1 Tbsp. butter
1 tsp. dry mustard or
    1 tsp. curry powder

Mix together and boil for 1 minute. You can add 1 cup whipped cream if desired.

From: **Mrs. B's Historic
Lanesboro Inn**
101 Parkway
Lanesboro, Minnesota

House Dressing

3 Tbsps. good mayonnaise
1 Tbsp. Dijon mustard
1 Tbsp. yellow mustard
3 Tbsps. red wine vinegar
2 cups oil
1 tsp. salt
½ tsp. freshly ground pepper
½ tsp. tarragon, fresh or dry

Mix the mayonnaise with the mustards, vinegar and spices until you have a smooth mixture.

Then add the oil a little at a time. Adjust the seasoning if necessary. If the mixture is a little too thick, add more oil.

From: **Chez Colette**
L'Hotel Sofitel
5601 West 78th Street
Bloomington, Minnesota

Fruit Dressing

1 tsp. celery seed or sesame seed
1 tsp. salt
½ tsp. paprika
½ tsp. dry mustard
⅓ cup vinegar
1 cup salad oil
1 cup honey
½ cup lemon juice

Mix all the dry ingredients. Add honey and lemon juice, stirring to paste consistency. Add vinegar and oil and beat two minutes. Yield: Approximately 1 quart.

From: **Michael's Restaurant**
15 South Broadway
Rochester, Minnesota

Orange Curry Dressing

1⅓ cups good mayonnaise,
  preferably homemade
⅓ cup honey
⅓ cup orange juice
½-1 tsp. white pepper
1-2 tsps. curry powder
½-1 tsp. dry mustard
1 tsp. garlic salt
½ tsp. nutmeg
1 tsp. orange bitters (optional)

Mix all ingredients in small bowl with wire whisk. Use larger quantity of spices for a stronger flavor.

This is an excellent dressing for sturdy greens like romaine lettuce, spinach, or watercress in combination with julienned red onions, mandarin oranges, and toasted pecans.

This dressing may be thinned with half and half if a more fluid product is desired.

From: **Jax Cafe**
University & 20th Avenue, N.E.
Minneapolis, Minnesota

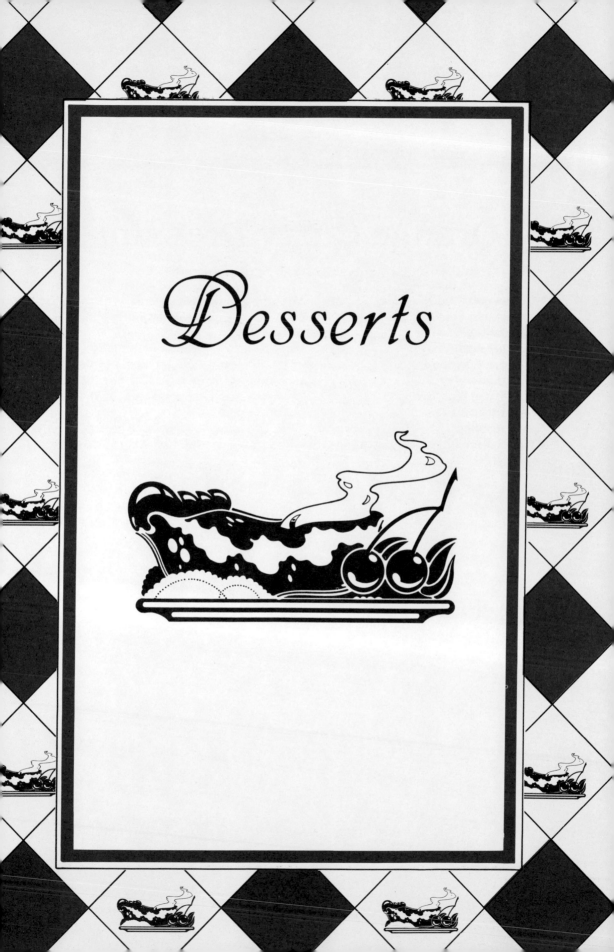

Desserts

Desserts

What is there to be said about desserts that has not already been said? "The dessert is said to be to the dinner what the madrigal is to literature—it is the light poetry of the kitchen." George Ellwanger said that in his book "Pleasures of the Table", published in 1903, and I think he summed up the subject pretty well.

However, each of us has different tastes in dessert. Some like fresh fruit and good cheeses; some are tempted only by chocolate, the richer and darker the better; some prefer pie over cake; some like souffles and creams. Minnesota's chefs have provided something for each taste.

See if there's not a variation on your favorite madrigal here.

Bananas Blagsvedt

Blagsvedt is the surname of a Norwegian family who have been our neighbors for 120 years in this country as they were in Norway before immigration.

Custard:
see Snow Pudding Recipe
*   on page 115*

Orange Sauce:
3 cups sugar, brown if desired,
*   or combination*
6 Tbsps. cornstarch
¾ tsp. salt
3 cups orange juice
2 Tbsps. lemon juice
1 cup water

Mix sugar, cornstarch and salt together. Add orange juice, lemon juice and water. Bring to a boil, stirring.

Mix the two sauces in a ratio of 1:1. Pour over sliced bananas and sprinkle with sugar mixed with dry, ground cardamom. Orange zest may be added as a garnish or grated bitter chocolate.

From: **Mrs. B's Historic
Lanesboro Inn**
101 Parkway
Lanesboro, Minnesota

Baked Apple with Apricot Rum Raisin Sauce

6 very large flavorful apples—
—Prairie Spy, McIntosh,
Cortland, or Yellow Delicious

1½ cups apricot preserves—
good quality, not too sweet
and not too thick
¾ cup golden raisins, plumped in
hot water and drained
¾ cup dark rum
1 cup apple juice

Preheat oven to 350 degrees.

Core apples, using a melon baller. Carefully peel the upper third of the apple, leaving a nice, neat line. Mix apricot preserves, plumped raisins and rum. Place cored apples in a glass baking dish and fill with the apricot mixture. Mix any remaining filling with apple juice and pour around the apples. Cover dish and bake until apples are spoon tender. Serve hot with yogurt, heavy cream or creme fraiche for breakfast, brunch or as dessert for a simple supper. Also good with a premium quality ice cream. Yield: 6 servings.

From: **Pam Sherman's Bakery & Cafe**
2914 Hennepin Avenue
Minneapolis, Minnesota

Mela Ripiena al'Avellane

4 large red apples
½ cup brown sugar
½ cup hazelnuts, finely chopped
2 tsps. cinnamon
1 pt. heavy cream
4 Tbsps. butter

Preheat oven to 350 degrees.

Keeping the apple whole, core the center out without going through the bottom. Mix brown sugar with the chopped hazelnuts and half of the cinnamon. Fill apple with this mixture and top with a tablespoon of butter. Bake in a 350-degree oven for 20-30 minutes. Let cool for at least an hour. Whip cream and

add sugar to taste with the remainder of cinnamon. Cover the apples with whipped cream and enjoy!!

From: **Pronto Ristorante**
Hyatt Regency Hotel
Minneapolis, Minnesota

Leola's Apple Dumplings

6 McIntosh, Cortland or other
  good, crisp apple

6 squares of pie pastry

sugar
cinnamon
butter

Sauce:
3 cups water
1½ cups sugar
¼ cup butter
½ tsp. cinnamon

Peel and core the apples, placing in a deep bowl of acidulated water (water to which you have added 2 tablespoons of lemon juice). This will keep the apples from browning.

Roll out the pie crust dough and cut into 6 squares, large enough to wrap around the apples. Place apple in the center of each square. In the cored apple, add equal parts sugar and cinnamon until half full. Add ½ teaspoon of butter and fill up with sugar and cinnamon. Wrap apples by bringing points of dough together and gently pressing the edges together. If edges will not stick, dab a little milk on edges and then press together. Put in baking pan, being sure dumplings don't touch each other.

Combine the water, sugar, butter and cinnamon for the sauce in a saucepan. Bring to a boil, boil for 1 minute. Then pour over apples. Bake in a preheated 350-degree oven for approximately 1 hour. Yield: 6 servings.

From: **The Grant House**
Fourth and Bremer
Rush City, Minnesota

Charlotte aux Fraises

This may be made in a souffle mold or simply as a round cake.

Ladies' Fingers:
3 eggs
⅓ cup sugar
½ cup flour
powdered sugar

Preheat oven to 400 degrees.

Blend egg yolks and sugar until creamy and light. Fold in flour and beaten egg whites. Push out of pastry bag in finger shapes as long as your souffle mold is deep. Bake 3-5 minutes. Top with powdered sugar.

Genoise:
4 eggs
⅔ cup sugar
⅞ cup flour

Preheat oven to 375 degrees.

Beat eggs and sugar in the top of a double boiler until tripled in volume. Don't let the sides of the pan get hot so the mixture gets hot. Beat until consistency is silky and you can form ribbons. Fold in flour. Pour into buttered and floured cake pan. Bake 12-15 minutes. Remove from pan; let cool. Slice in half lengthwise.

Strawberry Cream:
1 cup strawberry pulp
juice of ½ lemon
1 Tbsp. gelatin
3 Tbsps. strawberry liqueur
2 cups cream, whipped
2 egg whites
½ cup sugar

Strawberry Syrup:
½ cup strawberry pulp
⅓ cup sugar
¼ cup water
1½ Tbsps. Kirsch

Strawberry Jelly:
½ cup water
⅔ cup sugar
¾ cup strawberry pulp
2½ ozs. gelatin

For the strawberry cream, put pulp and lemon juice in bowl and dissolve gelatin in mixture. Add in strawberry liqueur. Fold in whipped cream.

Beat egg whites with sugar until stiff and shiny. Fold into strawberry mixture.

For the strawberry syrup, cook first 3 ingredients; strain until clear. Add Kirsch at end.

For strawberry jelly, cook first 3 ingredients; strain. Add gelatin.

To assemble, place the ladies' fingers around the edge of the pan or mold, top side against the outside of the mold. Place a slice of Genoise on the bottom, trimming it to fit, and saturate it with the strawberry syrup. Garnish with the strawberry charlotte cream and chill for 5-10 minutes.

Top with fresh strawberries, cover with remaining half of the strawberry charlotte cream. Place the other Genoise over the top, saturate it with strawberry syrup. Spread the whipped cream over the top. Chill thoroughly

Whipped Cream:
2 cups heavy cream
3 Tbsps. sugar

and then remove from the sides of the mold.

When you are ready to serve, top with the strawberry jelly and decorate with 1 or 2 strawberries dipped in jelly and 3 leaves made with green almond paste.

From: **Chez Colette**
L'Hotel Sofitel
5601 West 78th Street
Bloomington, Minnesota

Chocolate Mousse Cake

10 oz. semi-sweet chocolate
1 tsp. instant coffee
10 oz. unsalted butter
1½ cups sugar
6 egg yolks
6 egg whites

Preheat oven to 350 degrees.

Put chocolate and coffee in the top of a double boiler. Melt chocolate, stirring until smooth.

Cream the butter and sugar until light and fluffy. Add egg yolks one at a time, beating well each time. Add slightly cooled chocolate and mix well.

Beat egg whites until they form soft peaks. Add egg whites to chocolate mixture. Pour half the mixture into a well greased 12″ springform pan. Bake for 1 hour. Cool. Center will sink in. Add the other half batter to the center of cooled cake. Cake may be frozen at this point and warmed to room temperature before serving. Top with chopped pecans or walnuts. Yield: 10-12 servings.

From: **Trumpets**
Butler Square,
100 North Sixth Street
Minneapolis, Minnesota

Apricot Cheesecake

1½ cups graham cracker crumbs
⅓ cup butter, melted
⅓ cup sugar
4 oz. dried apricots
1½ cups water
1 cup sugar
2 Tbsps. lemon juice, fresh
2 lbs. cream cheese
⅛ tsp. salt
1¾ cups sugar
5 eggs
1¼ tsps. vanilla extract
2 cups sour cream
½ cup sugar
1½ tsps. vanilla extract

Preheat oven to 350 degrees.

Combine graham cracker crumbs, melted butter and ⅓ cup sugar and press into the bottom of a 9" springform pan.

Put apricots, water, one cup sugar and lemon juice in a heavy saucepan. Boil together until the apricots are soft. Remove from heat and beat until smooth or nearly so. Set aside to cool.

Beat the cream cheese, softened at room temperature, with salt and 1¾ cups sugar. Add eggs one at a time and blend until very smooth. Add the vanilla extract and apricot mixture and pour into springform pan.

Bake for 1 hour or until a knife or cake tester inserted in the center comes out clean.

Beat sour cream, sugar and vanilla extract together thoroughly and pour on top of cheesecake that has been allowed to cool for 10 minutes. Return to oven and bake for another 10 minutes.

Cool finished cheesecake completely and then refrigerate for 3 hours before serving. Yield: 1 cheesecake.

From: **Naniboujou Lodge**
Hwy. 61
(Star Route 1, Box 505)
Grand Marais, Minnesota

Fragoli con Zabaglione di Sciampagna

½ tsp. flour
¼ lb. sugar
8 egg yolks
¼ bottle champagne
  (inexpensive)
3 pts. fresh strawberries

Mix flour and sugar in a metal mixing bowl with whisk. Add egg yolks, one at a time, mixing thoroughly. Gradually add champagne, stirring constantly until the mixture is thick. Do not stop stirring.

Pour sauce into a chilled stainless steel bowl. Place in refrigerator. Stir sauce every ten minutes until completely chilled.

While sauce chills, slice strawberries.

Serve strawberries in individual bowls, top each with sauce.

From: **Figlio's**
3001 Hennepin Avenue
Minneapolis, Minnesota

Galatoboureko

1 qt. milk
1 cup farina
¾ cup butter
8 eggs
½ cup sugar
12 sheets phyllo dough

Syrup:
2 cups sugar
1 cup water
3 slices lemon rind

Preheat oven to 350 degrees.

Combine milk, farina and ½ cup of the butter. Bring to a boil, stirring to keep from sticking. Set mixture aside to cool. When slightly cooled, add beaten eggs and sugar to mixture. Layer 6 sheets of phyllo dough in a well buttered 11" x 14" baking pan, buttering each sheet of dough with the remaining ¼ cup melted butter. Add mixture to baking dish. Then layer 6 additional sheets of phyllo, buttering each sheet.

For syrup, combine the sugar and water and bring to a boil to thicken. Add lemon rinds.

Bake the egg and phyllo mixture for 1 hour, covered with baking paper. The last 20 minutes, bake at 325 degrees. Remove from oven and spoon syrup over egg and phyllo mixture. Cut into desired pieces.

From: **Michael's Restaurant**
15 South Broadway
Rochester, Minnesota

Mrs. B's Snow Pudding

A family tradition for Christmas Eve supper—Use your best wide, low glass bowl to serve this pudding. It's best by candlelight!

1½ cups milk, scalded
2 eggs, beaten
¼ cup sugar
½ tsp. vanilla extract
½ tsp. almond extract

Snowballs:
2 egg whites
¼ cup sugar
¼ tsp. almond extract

For the custard gradually add the hot, scalded milk to the eggs which have been beaten with the sugar, stirring rapidly. Return mixture to the burner and cook carefully until metal stirring spoon "coats"—not a moment longer! Strain, if necessary, and add flavorings. Chill, covered. When chilled, pour thick custard into chilled glass bowl and float snowballs of egg whites on top. Keep chilled until ready to serve. One snowball for each serving.

To make the snowballs, beat egg whites until fluffy. Add in sugar and extract, continuing to beat until stiff and shiny. Drop or slide snowballs into hot, lightly salted water in a wide saucepan. Should make 6-8 snowballs. Poach, covered, for 3-5 minutes. Uncover, drain and place on chilled custard.

From: **Mrs. B's Historic
Lanesboro Inn**
101 Parkway
Lanesboro, Minnesota

Baked Cream
with Fresh Fruit

8 egg yolks
4 eggs
1 cup sugar
1 tsp. vanilla extract
1 tsp. salt
1 qt. cream
1½-2 cups fresh fruit,
    any combination of berries,
    bananas, etc.

Preheat oven to 300 degrees.

In a mixing bowl combine egg yolks and whole eggs with sugar, vanilla extract and salt. Whip ingredients thoroughly until well blended. Slowly mix in cream until texture is smooth. Pour mixture into 12 lightly greased individual baking dishes or custard cups. Distribute the fresh, sliced fruits on top of the egg mixture and bake for approximately 30-40 minutes in the oven. Remove from oven and chill thoroughly before serving.

Optional—After chilling, sprinkle a small amount of brown sugar on top of each custard and place under a preheated broiler and glaze sugar for about 30-60 seconds; serve immediately.

From: **L'Etoile Restaurant**
The St. Paul Hotel
350 Market Street
St. Paul, Minnesota

Storybook Pudding

2-3 loaves French bread
8 eggs
1 cup milk
²/₃ cup cream
½ cup sugar
1 tsp. vanilla extract
½ tsp. almond extract
½ tsp. ginger
1 tsp. nutmeg
1 tsp. cinnamon
1 tsp. ground cloves
2 oz. chocolate chips
¼ cup walnuts, chopped

Cut or tear the bread into ¾-1½" cubes.

Mix all other ingredients, except nuts and chocolate chips, together, beating well. Pour over bread cubes in large bowl. Cover and refrigerate overnight.

Grease a 9" x 13" cake pan or 6 individual pie pans. Pour the custard bread mixture into pan, sprinkle top with chips and nuts. Bake in oven for 1 hour or until custard is set. May take less time for individual servings. Serve with good vanilla ice cream. Yield: 6 servings.

From: **Dudley Riggs'**
Cafe Espresso
1430 Washington Avenue, S.E.
Minneapolis, Minnesota

Swedish Settler Apple Pie

Filling:
2 cups canned, sliced apples
2 Tbsps. flour
¾ cup white sugar
1 egg
1 tsp. vanilla extract
1 cup sour cream
pinch of salt

Topping:
⅓ cup white sugar
⅓ cup flour
¾ tsp. cinnamon
¼ cup cold butter

1 10" unbaked pie shell

Preheat oven to 450 degrees.

Mix the filling ingredients together and pour into the pie shell.

Bake in oven for 20 minutes, then turn the temperature down to 350 degrees and bake for another 20 minutes.

For the topping, combine the first three ingredients in a small bowl and then cut the butter into them, using two knives or pastry blender. Remove the pie from the oven after it has baked for 40 minutes, sprinkle the topping over the pie and bake for an additional 20 minutes at 350 degrees. Yield: 1 pie serving 6-8 people.

From: **Fitger's Inn**
600 East Superior Street
Duluth, Minnesota

Cajon Pie

10 eggs
¼ cup vanilla extract
3 cups sugar
2 cups pastry flour
¾ lb. butter
3 cups chocolate chips
2 cups walnuts

Preheat oven to 325 degrees.

Beat eggs and vanilla together until thick and lemon colored. Add sugar and beat mixture until thick and creamy. Add flour and mix well. Cut up butter in small pieces, add to mixture, then blend well. Pour into greased 9" pie plates. Bake for 20 minutes. Add chips and walnuts and bake for another 20 minutes. Check pies, turn oven a little

lower and continue baking another 15 minutes. Cool about 20-25 minutes, then put plastic bags over them to cool completely. Yield: 3 pies.

From: **Michael's Restaurant**
15 South Broadway
Rochester, Minnesota

Chocolate Silk Pie

Crust:
⅓ cup butter, softened
1 cup powdered sugar
2½ ozs. unsweetened chocolate, melted
1 cup crushed Ritz type crackers

Filling:
2 cups powdered sugar
1 cup butter, softened
4 eggs, separated
3½ ozs. unsweetened chocolate, melted and cooled
1 tsp. vanilla extract

For the crust, cream butter and sugar; add chocolate and crackers. Press into a 9" pie tin, building up sides.

For the filling, cream sugar and butter together until light. Add egg yolks and beat until fluffy. Add chocolate and vanilla extract. Mix. Beat egg whites until stiff. Fold into chocolate mixture, being sure to mix well but not deflating egg whites. Spoon filling into crust. Refrigerate at least 2 hours. Serve with whipped cream.

This will keep refrigerated 4-5 days and may be frozen for 1 month, if well covered.

From: **W.A. Frost & Company**
374 Selby Avenue
St. Paul, Minnesota

Tarte au Citron

Sweet Pastry Dough:
1¾ cups flour
½ tsp. salt
½ cup sugar
4½ oz. sweet butter
1 egg yolk
2 Tbsps. water

Lemon Cream:
2 lemons
½ lb. butter
1 cup sugar
5 eggs
3 Tbsps. flour
1 Tbsp. cornstarch or arrowroot

Preheat oven to 350 degrees.

Using a pastry blender, blend flour, salt and sugar with butter until mixture resembles coarse cornmeal. Add egg yolk and water, blending all together. Roll out dough and put in a 9″ or 10″ tart pan, pricking with a fork. Put dried beans in a piece of foil in the shell and bake for 15 minutes. Remove from the oven.

Grate both lemons and put the rinds and lemon juice in a bowl. Add the melted butter, sugar and eggs and blend well. When smooth, add the flour and cornstarch or arrowroot. Whip the lemon cream in a double boiler until it begins to increase in volume. Pour into the shell and bake for 15 minutes. Yield: 10 servings.

From: **Chez Colette**
L'Hotel Sofitel
5601 West 78th Street
Bloomington, Minnesota

Tarte à l'Orange

Sweet Pastry Dough:
see Tarte au citron

Oranges:
1¼ lbs. oranges
1 cup water
2½ cups sugar

Creme Patisserie:
2 cups milk
2 Tbsps. grated orange zest
3 egg yolks
½ cup sugar
⅓ cup flour
¼ cup Grand Marnier

Make dough according to directions for Tarte au Citron. After baking for 15 minutes with beans in shell, remove beans and bake another 5-10 minutes.

Slice oranges in thin, even slices. Put the slices in a large saucepan and cover with the sugar. Add the water and simmer, covered, over a very low heat for 1 hour.

To prepare the creme patisserie, bring the milk to a boil with the orange zest. Strain. Beat the egg yolks, sugar and flour in a bowl. Pour the strained milk into the eggs, stirring constantly. Bring to a second boil, then flavor the cream with Grand Marnier. Strain the orange slices. Reduce the syrup the oranges were cooked in and reserve.

Pour the cream into the shell, then place the orange slices over the cream and glaze with the reduced syrup. Yield: 10 servings.

From:

Chez Colette
L'Hotel Sofitel
5601 West 78th Street
Bloomington, Minnesota

Mississippi Mud Pie

1 9" chocolate pie crust

1 pt. soft serve ice milk
½ oz. Amaretto
½ oz. coffee liqueur
1 cup chopped walnuts
1 pkg. chocolate mousse
1½ cups hot fudge sauce
whipped cream

Mix up the chocolate mousse, refrigerate. Mix liqueurs into the ice milk, pour into the crust and freeze. Ten minutes before serving, spread fudge over soft serve mixture, followed by mousse. Sprinkle nuts on top and spread whipped cream over all. Cut into 8 servings.

Chocolate Pie Crust

1½-2 cups chocolate
  wafer crumbs
6 Tbsps. melted butter

Pour the melted butter into the chocolate crumbs. Mix thoroughly. Put into 9" pie pan, press another pie pan on top to conform crust to sides of pan. Chill thoroughly.

From: **The Pirate's Cove**
7215 N.E. River Road
Sauk Rapids, Minnesota

Walnut Ice Cream Pie

2 egg whites
¼ cup sugar
1¼ cups finely chopped walnuts

Caramel Sauce:
¼ cup butter
1 cup brown sugar, finely packed
½ cup heavy cream
1 tsp. vanilla extract

Preheat oven to 400 degrees.

Beat egg whites until soft peaks form. Beat sugar in slowly, 1 tablespoon at a time, beating until stiff. Gently fold in walnuts. Butter 9" pie pan and spread mixture on bottom and up the sides of the pan. Bake for 10 minutes. Cool. Cut into 8 servings. Remove from pan. Fill each slice with vanilla ice cream.

Melt butter and sugar together. Mix well, remove from heat. Add cream. Return to heat and bring to boil, mixing well. Add vanilla extract. Cool slightly and spoon over ice cream. Yield: 8 servings.

From: **Kavanaugh's Restaurant**
2300 Kavanaugh Drive, S.W.
Brainerd, Minnesota

Raspberry Souffle

Souffle Base:
1½ oz. bread flour
1½ oz. butter
1½ oz. sugar

1 cup milk
1 tsp. vanilla extract
souffle base
4 egg yolks
5 egg whites
1½ oz. sugar
2 oz. raspberry liqueur
½ pt. raspberries,
   roughly chopped

Preheat oven to 400 degrees.

For souffle base, rub ingredients together to form a smooth paste, set aside.

Scald milk with vanilla extract. Add souffle base, blending well and whip with a fine wire whisk. Cook gently for 2 minutes, add egg yolks, one at a time, mixing well after each addition and cook until thick. Remove from heat and place mixture in stainless steel bowl. Add and whip in raspberry liqueur and fresh raspberries gently. Beat egg whites with sugar until very stiff but not dry. Pour egg whites over base mixture and gently fold them together with a rubber spatula until blended well. Do not overmix. Fill a souffle dish, buttered and dredged in sugar to within half inch of the rim. Sprinkle heavily with confectioner's sugar and bake approximately 25 minutes. Serve immediately with English vanilla cream.

From: **L'Etoile Restaurant**
The St. Paul Hotel
350 Market Street
St. Paul, Minnesota

Brandied Apricot Sauce

1 lb. apricot preserves
3 oz. whole butter
6 oz. brandy
¼ cup raisins

Melt butter and add to remaining ingredients, mix well and store in covered container in refrigerator for up to 4 weeks.

From: **Muffuleta in the Park**
2260 Como Avenue
St. Paul, Minnesota

Peanut Butter Cookies

1 cup shortening
1⅔ cups peanut butter
1 cup brown sugar
1 cup white sugar
1 tsp. vanilla extract
2 eggs
1½ tsps. baking soda
3⅔ cups flour, sifted

Preheat oven to 350 degrees.

Cream together shortening, peanut butter and sugars. Add eggs, vanilla extract and sifted flour and baking soda. Roll into balls about 1″ in diameter. Place on baking sheet, flatten with fork dipped in water to make crisscross pattern. Bake for 15 minutes.

From: **The Palmer House**
500 Sinclair Lewis Avenue
Sauk Centre, Minnesota

Linzer Cookies

1 egg
1 egg yolk
1 Tbsp. Kirsch
½ tsp. lemon zest, chopped
½ lb. unsalted butter
1½ cups sugar
2 cups pastry flour
⅔ cup cocoa
2 Tbsps. cinnamon
¼ tsp. ground cloves
¼ tsp. salt
2 cups ground almonds
  or hazelnuts
1 jar raspberry jam, best quality

Preheat oven to 350 degrees.

Cream butter and sugar, add egg and yolk and Kirsch. Stir in all other dry ingredients and form into 1″ balls. Make a depression in each ball with your finger and fill with ½ teaspoon raspberry jam. Bake on greased cookie sheets for 12 minutes. Yield: 7 dozen.

From:
**Pam Sherman's
Bakery & Cafe**
2914 Hennepin Avenue
Minneapolis, Minnesota

Inns & Restaurants

The numbers in parentheses after the name of the restaurant refer to the pages on which recipes from each establishment appear.

The Anderson House
333 West Main Street
Wabasha 55981
612/565-4524
MN toll free: 800/862-9702
No credit cards
(3, 17, 18, 20, 71, 87, 93, 94)

Treats, Ltd.
The Archer House
212 Division Street
Northfield 55057
507/663-0050
Credit cards: V, MC
(6, 43, 56, 67, 99)

Clyde's on the St. Croix
Bayport 55003
612/439-6554
Reservations advisable
Credit cards: V, MC, AE
(25, 65, 89)

East Bay Hotel
Grand Marais 55604
218/387-2800
Reservations advisable
No credit cards
(22, 76)

Fitger's Inn
600 East Superior Street
Duluth 55082
218/722-8826
Reservations advisable
Credit cards: V, MC, DC, AE, CB
(75, 78, 118)

The Grant House
Fourth and Bremer (Box 87)
Rush City 55069
612/358-4717
Reservations advisable
Credit cards: V, MC
(21, 109)

The Hubbell House
SH 57
Mantorville 55955
507/635-2331
Reservations advised
Credit cards: V, MC, AE, CB
(56)

Kavanaugh's Restaurant
2300 Kavanaugh Drive, S.W.
Brainerd 56401
218/829-5226
Reservations advised
Credit cards: V, MC
(68, 88, 123)

The Lowell Inn
102 North Second Street
Stillwater 55082
612/439-1100
Reservations necessary
Credit cards: V, MC, AE, DC
(19, 23, 92)

Mrs. B's Historic Lanesboro Inn
101 Parkway
Lanesboro 55949
507/467-2154
Reservations necessary
No credit cards
(3, 11, 24, 25, 60, 90, 91, 102, 107, 115)

INNS & RESTAURANTS

Michael's Restaurant
15 South Broadway
Rochester
507/288-2020
Reservations advised
Credit cards: V, MC, AE, DC, CB
(57, 72, 103, 114, 118)

Naniboujou Lodge
Hwy. 61 (Star Route 1, Box 505)
Grand Marais 55604
218/387-2688
Reservations necessary
Credit cards: V, MC, AE, DC, CB
Summer season:
    mid-May through mid-October
Winter season:
    selected weekends post-Christmas
    through mid-March
(112)

The Palmer House
500 Sinclair Lewis Avenue
Sauk Centre 56732
612/352-3431
Reservations advisable
No credit cards
(62, 66, 125)

The Pirate's Cove
7215 N.E. River Road
Sauk Rapids 56379
612/252-8400
Reservations appreciated
Credit cards: V, MC, AE, DC
(5, 48, 84, 122)

Stable's Supper Club
Richway Drive, West
Albert Lea 56007
507/373-8787
Reservations advised
Credit cards: V, MC
(26)

The Thayer Hotel
Hwy. 55
Annandale 55302
612/274-3371
Reservations advisable
Credit cards: V, MC
(92)

The Trout Haus
14536 West Freeway Drive
Forest Lake 55025
612/464-2964
No reservations
Credit cards: V, MC
(36, 79)

MINNEAPOLIS-ST. PAUL

Alfredo's
Park Square Court
400 Sibley Street
St. Paul
612/221-0551
Reservations advised
Credit cards: V, MC, AE, DC, CB
(8)

The Blue Horse
1355 University Avenue
St. Paul
612/645-8101
Reservations advised
Credit cards: V, MC, AE, DC, CB
(76, 98)

Caravan Serai
2046 Pinehurst Avenue
St. Paul
612/690-1935
Reservations
Credit cards: V, MC, AE, DC, CB
(30, 39, 55)

Chez Colette
L'Hotel Sofitel
5601 West 78th Street
Bloomington 55420
612/835-0126
Reservations advised
Credit cards: V, MC, AE, DC, CB
(31, 41, 103, 110, 120, 121)

Dudley Riggs' Cafe Espresso (late night)
1430 Washington Avenue, S.E.
Minneapolis
612/338-5534
No Reservations
Credit cards: V, MC, AE, DC, CB
(44, 117)

The Egg and I (breakfast & lunch)
2704 Lyndale Avenue S.
Minneapolis
612/872-7282
No reservations
No credit cards
(4)

L'Etoile Restaurant
The St. Paul Hotel
350 Market Street
St. Paul
612/292-9292
Reservations necessary
Credit cards: V, MC, AE, DC, CB
(29, 32, 25, 59, 82, 116, 124)

The Fifth Season
Marriott City Center Hotel
30 7th Street S.
Minneapolis
612/349-4000
Reservations necessary
Credit cards: V, MC, AE, CB, DC
(34, 45, 64)

Figlio's
3001 Hennepin Avenue
Minneapolis
612/822-1688
Reservations advisable
Credit cards: V, MC, AE, DC, CB
(5, 49, 113)

The 510
510 Groveland Avenue
Minneapolis
612/874-6440
Reservations necessary
Credit cards: V, MC, AE, DC, CB
(42, 46, 69, 97)

W.A. Frost & Company
374 Selby Avenue
St. Paul
612/224-5715
Reservations advisable
Credit cards: V, MC, AE, DC, CB
(7, 101, 119)

Jax Cafe
University & 20th Avenue, N.E.
Minneapolis
612/789-7297
Reservations advisable
Credit cards: V, MC, AE, DC, CB
(40, 47, 58, 60, 80, 81, 83, 100, 104)

Muffuletta in the Park
2260 Como Avenue
St. Paul
612/333-5900
Reservations advisable
Credit cards: V, MC, AE, DC, CB
(7, 83, 125)

also **Muffuletta on the Lake**
739 Lake Street
Wayzata 55391
612/475-3636
(7, 83, 125)

Primavera
The Atrium
International Market Square
275 Market Street
Minneapolis
612/339-8000
Reservations advisable
Credit Cards: V, MC, AE
(9, 10)

Pronto Ristorante
Hyatt Regency Hotel
Minneapolis
612/333-4414
Reservations necessary
Credit cards: V, MC, AE
(12, 63, 108)

Pam Sherman's Bakery & Cafe
2914 Hennepin Avenue
Minneapolis
612/824-0604
No reservations
No credit cards
(13, 14, 108, 126)

Trumpets
Butler Square
100 North Sixth Street
Minneapolis
612/340-1850
Reservations advisable
Credit cards: V, MC
(66, 68, 111)

Index

A

APPETIZERS 27-36
Gravad Lox with Mustard Dill Sauce 29
Kofta 30
Moules Mariniere 31
Pheasant Pate en Croute 32
Cornet of Salmon "Ciboulette" 34
Potpourri of Salmon 35
Smoked Troute Mousse 36
Apples—
Baked, with Apricot Rum
    Raisin Sauce 108
Mela Ripiena al'Avellane 108
Leola's Dumplings 109
Swedish Settler Pie 118
Stuffing for Rosy Glazed Goose 71
Apricot—
Brandied Sauce 125
Cheesecake 112
Rum Raisin Sauce 108
Layered Pork Loin with Fruit 60

B

Bananas—
Blagsvedt 107
Beef—
Curry 55

Tips in Wild Rice 56
Madras Curry 56
Pepper Steak 57
Roast Tenderloin of, with Five
    Peppercorns and Dijon Hollandaise . . . 58
Biscuits—
Plum 17
BREAD, ROLLS & MUFFINS 15-26
Plum Biscuits 17
Lemon Cream Nut Bread 18
Swiss Pear Bread 19
Italian Pepper and Crackling Bread 20
Limpa Bread 21
Swedish Raisin Rye 22
Crescent Rolls 23
Currant Scones 24
Van's Garlic Toast 26
Sweetened Butter 25
Cinnamon Honey Butter 25
Bread—
Garlic Toast, Van's 26
Italian Pepper and Crackling 20
Lemon Cream Nut 18
Limpa 21
Swedish Rye Raisin 22
Swiss Pear 19
Broccoli—
Egg Bake 88
Quiche 5

BRUNCH & LUNCHEON 1-14
   Five Star Brunch 3
   Goatmilk Yogurt Pancakes.............. 3
   Kamikaze Pancakes 4
   Broccoli Quiche 5
   Capellini con Gamberetti 5
   Chicken Breast in a Package 6
   Chili with Beef, Pork and Chicken....... 7
   Clam Linguini 7
   Linguini con Vongole 8
   Ragout of Lobster and
     Seasonal Vegetables.................. 9
   Lobster Stock 10
   Poppy Seed Spatzle................... 11
   Ravioli con Zucca 12
   Vegetarian Stuffed Peppers 13
   Tomato Sauce 14
Butter—
   Cinnamon Honey..................... 25
   Sweetened 25

C

Charlotte—
   aux Fraises.......................... 110
Cheese—
   Bell, Soup 40
Cheesecake—
   Apricot.............................. 112
Chicken—
   Breast in a Package................... 6
   Champagne Chicken Breasts 65
   Curry 66
   Mediterranean, Soup 43
   Pauline 66
   Punjabi 67
   Salads—
     Oriental 98
     Tarragon 99
   a la Seaver 68
   Stuffed Chicken Breast 68
Chili—
   with Beef, Pork, and Chicken 7
Chocolate—
   Mousse Cake 111
   Pie Crust........................... 119
   Silk Pie 119
Clams—
   Clam Linguini 7
   Linguini con Vongole 8
Cookies—
   Linzer 126
   Peanut Butter 125
Cream—
   Baked, with Fresh Fruit 116
   Lemon for Tarte au Citron 120

   Patisserie for Tarte a l'Orange 121
   Strawberry for Charlotte 110
Cucumber—
   Afghan, Soup......................... 39
Curry—
   Chicken............................. 66
   Beef................................ 55
   Madras Beef 56

D

DESSERTS 105-126
   Bananas Blagsvedt 107
   Baked Apples with
     Apricot Rum Raisin Sauce 108
   Mela Ripiena al'Avellane 108
   Leola's Apple Dumplings 109
   Charlotte aux Fraises 110
   Chocolate Mousse Cake 111
   Apricot Cheesecake 112
   Fragoli con Zabaglione
     di Sciampagna 113
   Galatoboureko 114
   Mrs. B's Snow Pudding 115
   Baked Cream with Fresh Fruit 116
   Storybook Pudding 117
   Swedish Settler Apple Pie 118
   Cajon Pie........................... 118
   Chocolate Silk Pie 119
   Tarte au Citron 120
   Tarte a l'Orange 121
   Mississippi Mud Pie 122
   Walnut Ice Cream Pie 123
   Raspberry Souffle 124
   Brandied Apricot Sauce 125
   Peanut Butter Cookies 125
   Linzer Cookies 126
Duck—
   Grilled Breast of, with Wild Mushrooms
     and Green Peppercorns............... 69
   Wild Rice and Duck Salad
     with Chutney Dressing 100

E

Eggs—
   Broccoli and, Bake 88
   Five Star Brunch 3

F

FISH & SEAFOOD 73-84
   Beer Batter for Fish 75
   Lake Superior Fish Cakes 76
   Lobster Medallions with
     Wild Mushrooms 76

Oysters Fitgers 78
Broiled Rainbow Trout 79
Trout Florentine 80
Trout Frangelica 81
Grand Marnier 81
Grilled Salmon with Raspberry
   Beurre Blanc Sauce 82
Grilled Roma Salmon
Sole with Minted Mousseline Sauce 83
Stuffed Sole 84

G

Galatoboureko 114
Goose—
Roast with Apple Stuffing/Rosy Glaze ... 71

H

Hollandaise—
Dijon 58

I

Inns and Restaurants, List 127
Involtina de Vitello alla Genovese 63
Italian Meats and Cheeses 53

J

K

Kofta 30

L

Lamb—
Loin of Lamb in Puff Pastry 59
Lamb Chops Raymond 60
Linguini—
Clam 7
con Vongole 8
Lobster—
Bisque de Homard 41
Medallions of, with Wild Mushrooms 76
Ragout of, with Seasonal Vegetables 9
Stock 10

M

MEAT & POULTRY 51-72
Italian Meats and Cheeses 53
Beef Curry 55
Beef Tips in Wild Rice 56
Madras Beef Curry...................... 56

Pepper Steak 57
Roast Tenderloin of, with Five
   Peppercorns and Dijon Hollandaise ... 58
Loin of Lamb in Puff Pastry 59
Lamb Chops Raymond................... 60
Layered Pork Loin with Fruit 60
Pork Medallions in
   Mushroom Beer Gravy 62
Involtini di Vitello alla Genovese 63
Veal Wellington with
   Capacola and Spinach 64
Champagne Chicken Breasts 65
Chicken Curry 66
Chicken Pauline 66
Punjabi Chicken........................ 67
Chicken a la Seaver 68
Stuffed Chicken Breast 68
Grilled Duck 69
Rosy Glazed Goose
   with Apple Stuffing 71
Pheasant in Sour Cream Sauce 72
Medallions—
Lobster, with Wild Mushrooms 76
Pork, with Mushroom Beef Gravy 62
Moules (Mussels)—
Mariniere 31
Saffron Mussel Soup 45
Mousseline—
Minted Sauce for Sole 83
Mustard—
Dill Sauce for Gravad Lox 1
Dijon Hollandaise for
   Tenderloin of Beef 58

N

O

P

Pancakes—
Goatmilk Yogurt........................ 3
Kamikaze 4
Pastry Dough—
Sweet, for Tartes 120
Pate—
Pheasant............................... 4
Peas—
and Beet Greens....................... 90
Sugar Snap, Cream Soup 46
Peanut Butter—
Cookies 125
Pheasant—
Pate en Croute 4
in Sour Cream Sauce 72

Pie—
Swedish Settler Apple 118
Cajon 118
Chocolate Silk 119
Tarte au Citron 120
Tarte a l'Orange 121
Mississippi Mud...................... 122
Walnut Ice Cream 123
Poppy Seeds—
Spatzle............................. 11
Pork—
Layered Pork Loin with Fruit 60
Pork Medallions in
Mushroom Beer Gravy 62
Potatoes—
Butter Baked 91
Twice Baked 92
Poultry—
see Chicken, Goose and Pheasant ... 65-72
Pudding—
Snow 115
Storybook.......................... 117

Q

Quiche—
Broccoli............................. 5

R

Ragout—
of Lobster with Seasonal Vegetables 9
Raspberry—
Beurre Blanc Sauce
with Grilled Salmon 82
Souffle 124
Ravioli—
con Zucca........................... 12
Roast—
Tenderloin of Beef with Five
Peppercorns and Dijon Hollandaise ... 58
Loin of Lamb in Puff Pastry 59
Layered Pork Loin with Fruit 60
Rolls—
Crescent 23

S

SALADS & SALAD DRESSINGS..... 95-104
Belgian Endive and Strawberry 97
Caesar Salad 98
Oriental Chicken 98
Tarragon Chicken 99
Wild Rice and Duck with
Chutney Dressing 100
Wild Rice and Smoked Turkey 101

Winter, for Minnesota
with Boiled Dressing 102
Chez Colette House Dressing 103
Fruit Dressing....................... 103
Orange Curry Dressing 104
Salmon—
Cornet of, "Ciboulette" 5
Gravad Lox 1
Grilled, with Raspberry
Beurre Blanc Sauce 82
Grilled Roma 83
Potpourri of 6
Sauce—
Americaine, for Lobster Medallions
with Wild Mushrooms 76
Cumberland for Pheasant Pate 32
Minted Mousseline for Sole 83
Mustard Dill for Gravad Lox............ 1
Orange for Bananas Blagsvedt 107
Raspberry Beurre Blanc
for Grilled Salmon 82
Rum Raisin for Baked Apples 108
Watercress for Potpourri of Salmon 35
Scones—
Currant 24
Souffle—
Raspberry 124
SOUPS 37-50
Afghan Cucumber 39
Bell Cheese 40
Bisque de Homard.................... 41
Fennel Cream 42
Mediterranean Chicken................ 43
Les Halles Style French Onion 44
Saffron Mussel 45
Sugar Snap Pea Cream 46
Cream of Wild Rice 47
Wild Rice........................... 48
Zuppa di Pane con Salcicce 49
Spinach—
Balls 93
Loin of Lamb in Puff Pastry 59
Veal Wellington with
Capacola & Spinach 64
Strawberry—
Belgian Endive and, Salad 97
Charlotte au Fraises 110
Fragoli con Zabaglione
di Sciampagna 113

T

Tomatoes—
Florentine........................... 94
Trout—
Mousse, Smoked 36

134

Turkey—
Smoked, Wild Rice Salad 101

U

V

Veal—
Involtini di Vitello alla Genovese 63
Veal Wellington with
   Capacola and Spinach 64
VEGETABLES 85-94
Barley Mushroom Casserole 87
Broccoli Egg Bake 88
Sherried Mushrooms 89
Peas and Beet Greens 90
Butter Baked Potatoes 91
Twice Baked Potatoes 92
Red Cabbage 92
Spinach Balls 93
Tomatoes Florentine 94

W

Walnut—
Ice Cream Pie 123

Wellington—
Veal, with Cappecola and Spinach 64
Wild Rice—
Beef Tips, in 56
Cream of, Soup 47
and Duck Salad
   with Chutney Dressing 100
Soup 48
and Smoked Turkey Salad 101

X

Y

Z

Zabaglione,
Fragoli con, di Sciampagna 113
Zuppa—see Soups